IF LIFE IS A JOURNEY,
THEN THE SOUL IS YOUR
GUIDING FORCE.

LEARN HOW TO . . .

- Hear your soul speaking to you
- Recognize the voice of your guardian angel
- Follow four exercises before breakfast to
  become more spiritual
- Find Lao-tzu's one path to integrity
- Carry out your first moral duty
- Free your innate creativity
- Transcend time
- Feel a magnificent inner peace as
  you connect with a Higher Power

THE
PORTABLE
PILGRIM

Seven Steps to Spiritual Enlightenment

SUSANNA McMAHON, PH.D.

A DELL TRADE PAPERBACK

A DELL TRADE PAPERBACK

Published by
Dell Publishing
a division of
Bantam Doubleday Dell Publishing Group, Inc.
1540 Broadway
New York, New York 10036

Library of Congress Cataloging in Publication Data
McMahon, Susanna.
    The portable pilgrim / Susanna McMahon.
        p.   cm.
    Includes bibliographical references and index.
    ISBN 0-440-50829-0
    1. Spiritual life.   2. Virtues.   I. Title.
BL624.M3984   1998
291.4′4—dc21   98-7074
                                                          CIP

Printed in the United States of America

Published simultaneously in Canada

December 1998

10 9 8 7 6 5 4 3 2 1

BVG

for Timothy
with love

ACKNOWLEDGMENTS

As always, I want to thank my family for putting up with me as I wrote and edited and rewrote and reedited this book. Thank you all for your patience, generosity, and spirituality in loving me even when I was absent or unavailable for weeks at a time. This is most true for my beloved Tim and Jennifer, but Catherine, Kelly, Mother, Nick, and Mike were also always understanding and supportive.

I am blessed with amazing friends; thank you all, again and again—in Spain, Elizabeth and David, Anne and Jesus, Judy, Betty and Alf; in Houston, Joanna and Andrew, Rita and Blair, Barbara and Rusty; in Texas, Beth and Paul and, of course and forever, Buzz and Gloria.

And again, much thanks to Margret McBride and her excellent staff, especially Winifred Golden. To my new editor at Dell, Mary Ellen O'Neill, I wish to give special thanks for her interest, concern, and understanding and for her invaluable help in turning my manuscript into this book.

There were two books that were especially valuable in the writing of this book. The first is Huston Smith's classic *The Religions of Man,* and the second is Neale Donald Walsch's recent publication *Conversations with God: An Uncommon Dialogue.* Since religion is not my area of expertise, I thank both these authors for making my life so much easier and giving this book validity. The quotations are theirs, the interpretations mine, and they have no responsibility for any misconceptions on my part.

Many of the religious ideas and concepts came from the five videotapes *The Wisdom of Faith with Huston Smith.* A Bill Moyers Special. Public Affairs Television, Inc. (For information call 800-257-5126.)

All the teaching stories were told to me by Dr. Walter "Buzz" O'Connell, director of the Natural High Center in Bastrop, Texas, with the exception of the one used in the chapter on creativity. This was told to me by John Coon, director of the Yoga Center in Houston, Texas.

Give me my scallop shell of quiet,
My staff of faith to walk upon,
My scrip of joy, immortal diet,
My bottle of salvation,
My gown of glory, hope's true gage,
And thus I'll take my pilgrimage.
                    —Sir Walter Raleigh

This be my pilgrimage and goal,
Daily to march and find
The secret phrases of the soul,
The evangels of the mind.
                    —John Drinkwater

CONTENTS

3. THE THIRD STEP: *Morality* 51

4. THE FOURTH STEP: *Creativity* 75

INTRODUCTION

A pilgrim is a traveler to a shrine or holy place or, even more simply, a wanderer. A pilgrimage is the journey made by a pilgrim or any long journey. If we think of ourselves as wanderers and our lives as long journeys, then by the simplest definitions, we are all pilgrims and our lives are pilgrimages. And when we begin the search for meaning in our lives, when we seek awareness of that which is good, important, and real, when we quest for the sacred—something grander than ourselves—then we truly become the more traditional definition of a pilgrim. Our journey toward meaning becomes our own personal voyage of discovery, the pilgrimage to our souls.

Nowadays very few of us, unless we are Muslims, think of actually going on a pilgrimage, but this was not always so. During the Middle Ages, and lasting for several centuries, more than half a million travelers each year went on holy treks. Christians had three possible places to journey: Rome, Jerusalem, and Santiago de Compostela in northern Spain. Rome was where Peter founded the Catholic Church, and those who traveled there were known as romeros. Jerusalem was where Christ was crucified and arose from the dead; these travelers were called palmers because they returned with palm branches. Only those who traveled to Santiago de Compostela, the shrine of St. James, defeater of the Moors and patron saint of Spain, could be called pilgrims, for this was by far the most hazardous and lengthy journey of the three.

Pilgrims undertook this challenging and dangerous trek for many reasons, the most common being to seek the spiritual or to find salvation. Warriors and knights often vowed to make a pilgrimage if they survived in battle. Clergy saw the pilgrimage as the ultimate quest for the Divine, the culmination of their holy lives. But there were also criminals, sentenced to either jail or pilgrimage, and there were always the thieves, beggars, and unsavory characters who went for financial gain and preyed on the devout as they traveled along. Also, there were merchants, architects, weavers, painters, and all manner of businessmen who perceived the journey as a marketplace. Finally, there were foreign agents and political spies. The composition of these early pilgrimages readily lends itself to comparison with modern life.

In the midst of those who are seeking the holy are always those who desire the profane; as a matter of fact, we are often personally caught in the battle between what we desire (our mortal dreams) and what we seek (our immortal souls). We are constantly being seduced and distracted by worldly desires, wealth, and comfort. We are trained to believe that happiness comes with pleasure, that security and safety come with money and possessions, and that there should be an easy, painless fix for all our problems and difficulties. We quickly become afraid of taking what we perceive as a painful path; we do not want our lives ever to be hard or unknown or unsure. Thus, we learn to view happiness as our right, status as our reward, and comfort as our due. Then, when we do achieve these desires, we are surprised that we still wonder what is missing. Where have we failed? Why do we want more, and what exactly is it that we are yearning for?

This is precisely the place to begin the pilgrimage. It is only when we find what we seek, when we achieve what we think we desire, that we become free to discover that there is more to us, more to life than what we have been taught. For it is when we have supposedly achieved "success" that we discover that what we have is not what we want and we must look farther afield. In short, we must journey to new territory. It is as if we have always traveled to our destination via a certain road and now this road is torn up and impassable. We don't know where to go, and we're no longer sure that we even want to go anymore. And this revelation is both frightening and frustrating, for it is not what we have been led to expect.

And it is now, in this state of confusion, that the soul has a chance to assert itself over the controlling ego and the noisy mind. The soul needs a quiet space in order to be heard; nothing stops the incessant chatter of the mind and the constant demands of the ego as surely as not knowing and being uncertain. Think of the ego as a hot-air balloon and of confusion as the pin that bursts the balloon. However, because we are familiar with the world of the ego and not at all comfortable with the soul's reality, we can easily become afraid and depressed in this new place, unless we understand the process. For we have spent years making sense of the physical world, we have listened to our minds, we have developed our egos to define us, we have fed, clothed, and exercised our bodies, and all the while we have ignored our souls. It seems to have taken all our time just to attend to the business of living in the world that we know, see, smell, and hear; how, then, can we have been expected to deal with something as mysterious and ambiguous as the soul?

What do we know of the soul? We have heard that it is our immortal essence, our spiritual force and moral nature, our vital and essential beingness, our connection to God. We know that it cannot be seen because it has no physical or material presence. It cannot be counted, weighed, measured, or replicated, so from a scientific point of view, it is easy to dismiss or ignore. If we have been curious about it, we may have read recent books that describe it as the part of ourselves that knows everything but desires a physical existence in order to experience that which is known but not yet felt. And that it contains the best of us and also our shadow or dark sides. We may have heard that the soul is the true driving force behind who we are, what we do, think, say, and feel and that it organizes all our experiences into our meanings. Yet we may be left wondering exactly how to tap into it, communicate with it, and allow it to guide us actively.

Discovering the soul is like learning to play bridge. The

only way to learn is to play, even though in the beginning you have no earthly idea what you are doing or why you are doing it. The rules of the game simply do not make sense until you have played for a while. Therefore, you must begin without understanding, but with the faith that one day it will all make sense. If you keep at it, one day everything falls into place and forms a cohesive and connected pattern of meaning. Thus, you have taken the risk to do something that makes no sense and to keep at it until it does. Your reward is that you become a bridge player; what was once so unclear and unfamiliar now seems natural, easy, and great fun.

Discovering the soul can also be compared with falling in love. You simply cannot imagine the experience until it has happened to you. You can hear about it and see it in others, but it is not a rational event that can be communicated or taught by normal teaching methods. The only way to understand the phenomenon is to experience it for yourself. This involves the element of risk, for falling in love means giving up your control, your illusions of safety, and your need for rational behavior. It means that your emotions override your usually dominant and powerful mind. You simply cannot think yourself into love; the only way to get there is to feel.

So it is with the soul. In order to discover your soul, you must allow it to override your rational mind and your insecure ego. Both are working hard to allow you some illusion of security, to order the world, to organize the chaos, and to give you definite boundaries by which you define yourself. They help you know exactly where you begin and end so that you can differentiate yourself as a unique and important individual in this confusing world. In doing so, they separate you from everything that is not you. And it is in this separation that your difficulties occur.

Separation is not the domain of the soul, for the soul is the connection to the Life Force, the Higher Power, God. It is also your connection to all living things. For in order to recognize your soul, you must simultaneously recognize the soul in others. Becoming aware of your goodness (soulfulness) is intimately connected to the awareness of the innate goodness in all being. Therefore, the pilgrimage to your own soul is the journey toward virtue, the awareness that goodness—God—exists in all things. It is the understanding that there is both mystery and revelation in every moment. It involves beginning without comprehension (similar to playing bridge) and experiencing without understanding (like falling in love).

Ultimately this is indeed a spiritual trip even if you have difficulty with the religious concepts of God, spirit, and soul. You do not have to believe in God to be a pilgrim, but you do need to believe in goodness. I have never met anyone who does not understand the latter, even when he finds it difficult to apply to himself. This book is about finding your virtue and living your goodness; I hope it will help you discover your soul and find the true meaning of your life. The only requirement is your ability to perceive your life as a pilgrimage and your willingness to take the risk and become a pilgrim.

This book is based on my own pilgrimage toward the soul. The path I present is the path of virtue, defined through seven modern and familiar characteristics inherent in all of us. There are many other paths equally as good as the one I have chosen. What I have selected is, first, a simple path, one that is both describable and livable. This does not mean it is easy, for simple and easy are not the same. But it does mean that it is available to anyone desiring the experience. My second criterion is that this is a practical path, one that can be understood and achieved by following the steps. Finally, it must be a valid path; therefore, I could not rely only upon my own interpretations and experiences. I have looked for validation from many sources, including religion, philosophy, psychology and psychiatry, artists, authors, and teachers. The ideas presented are not original, but I take full responsibility for the presentation.

The soul is generally considered to be within the domain of religion, and each religion offers instruction on what the soul is and how it is found. There seems to be consensus that the soul is or represents a connection to the Creator. Therefore, each religion can be considered as another path to the soul and ultimately to whatever we call our Creator: God, Allah, Yahweh, Jehovah, Buddha, Brahman, Atman, Ram, the Almighty or Higher Power.

The religious path that I am most familiar with is Christianity; because of my education and culture, it is natural for me to call the Creator God. However, in doing so, I do not mean to imply that my concept of God is preferable to any other one. Instinctively I believe that we are all referring to the same force—the same great Being, our highest source—no matter what name we use.

In each of the seven chapters of this book, I have emphasized one of the seven major world religions over the others. Each religion seems to lend itself particularly well to explaining or clarifying a specific virtue, although I recognize that every religion contains all the virtues. In writing this book, I intended not to be a proponent of any one religion but to be a presenter of something relevant about each of them. Perhaps my intent is best captured by the Hindu idea of the Supreme Being existing at the top of a mountain and each religion representing a different path to the top. If we spend our time running around the bottom of the mountain trying to convert others to our particular path, we do not get any closer to the top. In the end it is not nearly as important what path we choose as it is that we get on one and begin our personal journey upward.

I have taken some liberties with the concept of virtue and have chosen seven characteristics to describe a virtuous person in today's world. I deliberately chose not to rely upon the traditional cardinal virtues. This is because we seem over time to have lost a sense of connection to these qualities. In fact, when I began this book, I could not remember all of them, and in my limited investigation I could find no one else who could name all seven. (It is interesting that all of us found it much easier to list and resonate with the seven deadly sins!) With the help of my friendly librarian, the cardinal virtues are: justice, prudence, temperance, fortitude, faith, hope, and charity. Do you relate to these? I have chosen instead to deal with the following characteristics: objectivity, integrity, morality, creativity, spontaneity, generosity, and spirituality. I hope you can better identify with them. However, I discovered that there is a clear relationship between these modern virtues and the historical ones, and I have incorporated the two.

As a clinical psychologist I try to help clients accept and live the reality of their lives to the best of their abilities. The search for spirituality, the discovery of the soul, is a natural and inevitable progression of this work. For in discovering how best to cope with the reality of the external world, we must concern ourselves and become involved with the internal world. Thus, we discover another more meaningful reality: that we are indeed connected and related to a Higher Power, a Universal Consciousness. As soon as we begin to confront the ego-self and begin to constrain its power over us, we learn that we are not alone, that we are not separate, and that there is infinite power within the true Self. For once we subdue the ego, we come face-to-face with the soul, our connection to God.

The degree to which I subdue my ego
is the degree to which I am objective.

1

THE FIRST STEP:
Objectivity

"DO YOU PLAY poker?" the World War II veteran asked me one day during group therapy. I nodded yes.

"Well, you must be pretty lousy," and he laughed.

He was right (I am not a good poker player), but I did not understand how he knew that, and my face must have reflected my lack of comprehension. He went on to explain.

"In your therapy with us, you give away all the aces. If you were holding all four aces in a poker game, everyone at the table would know. Not only that, you would want to show them your hand right away before the pot got big. You gotta learn how to bluff."

This particular veteran was unusual for the fourth ward at the VA hospital in Houston; all the others on this ward were Vietnam veterans suffering from posttraumatic stress syndrome. However, in spite of his age and different experience of war, he was very similar to the others in his symptoms and his suffering. Like the Nam vets, he was trying to make some sense out of life; the easiest way for him to do this was to try to make life a game. After all, he had survived the most dangerous game of all. However, despite the frequent comparisons, life is really not a game because games have specified rules, clear and understood goals, recognizable and known endings, and some premise of fairness; even in war, truces are usually respected. This is not life.

Nonetheless, his comparison is relevant, for if life were like a game of poker and held four aces, the aces would be self-worth, unconditional love, awareness (actualization), and connection to the Whole (universal belonging). But life does not deal us these aces; we have to learn and discover them from our own experiences. We lose them if we bluff or try to hold on to them or hide them. They are not external to us, nor are they finite or limited; they are not found through competing with others. Furthermore, we cannot expect to get them simply by following the rules and playing fairly. We do not "win" when others lose; we are not dealt the aces simply by chance. For life is not fair, and it is not clear what "winning" at it entails.

Why is life like a pilgrimage?

Perhaps the more relevant analogy is that life is similar to a pilgrimage. Here it is understood that there is a goal—arriving at a specified destination—but the journey itself is expected to be difficult, full of challenges and dangers, and to take many years, perhaps even a lifetime. The purpose of the pilgrimage may be the most relevant similarity of all: The journey is undertaken in order to find the true Self and its connection to that which is greater than the self. By facing the dangers and overcoming the difficulties, the pilgrim discovers weaknesses and strengths, vanities and virtues, evil and goodness—in fact, everything that constitutes the complete Self. But in order to make these discoveries, we must become objective. We must learn to perceive realistically our Selves as they really are; we must recognize that the four aces are found internally and not achieved externally. They are part of our infinite potential rather than our finite achievements. They are realized in our eternal being rather than our worldly doing.

But, oh, how our subjective selves—our egos—want life to be a game rather than a pilgrimage. We desire the easy over the difficult. We want the rules to be clear, the goals to be simple, the playing fair and fun, and, above all, we want to win and be happy. We want to know that the ending will be successful. Perhaps we try to make life a game because we have learned to satisfy our wants and needs only from external sources. When we seek pleasure, fame, money, or power from the outer world, we often do so as players in a game: I win, you lose; I am powerful, you are weak; I am rich, you are poor; and so on.

And, if we believe that external things are the critical attributes of our lives, it is easy to lose ourselves in the satisfaction of these wants. When we do so, we have defined ourselves as mere players; we perceive ourselves solely as our roles or positions. Then it feels normal to treat life as the playing field of our fulfillment. That is when we lose our sense of wonder, our awe of the mystery, our hope for grace. Our subjective egos limit our worldview; they prevent us from beginning the pilgrimage.

What is objectivity?

Most simply, *objectivity* means that we become aware that there is a reality beyond our subjective selves. This reality exists both outside the self and deeply within it. Obviously it is much easier to be objective about an external reality than about an internal one. This is because the defining concept of *objectivity* is that it involves something external to or independent of our minds. It means that we are able to perceive an object as separate from ourselves. Being objective also means being able to perceive without bias or prejudice; again, this implies separation from our thoughts or feelings.

The idea of becoming objective with the self, then, is a contradiction, a paradox. For how can we objectively perceive ourselves when, by definition, the self is the definition of subjectivity? How can we become independent of our own minds, feelings, thoughts, or selves? Yet this is what we must do in order to become objective; we must move beyond our minds and feelings and even our physical bodies (our external selves). We move beyond not only by reaching out to an external and greater reality but also by going in to an internal one. It can be compared with studying ourselves with both a telescope and a microscope.

This journey within is the only answer to finding our true Selves, but it is difficult because it requires moving beyond our familiar constructions of the self, our egos. The *ego* can be defined as our sense of self-importance in relation to others. In other words, we must let go of the need for others to define us and journey inside to our deepest, darkest interiors in order to know who we really are. Our inner selves—our spirits, souls, and dark sides—are real; they do exist within us and are separate from and not limited by our egos. Yet our inner selves are constrained by our egos unless we develop objectivity and become aware of our true natures. Becoming objective about the reality of who we really are begins, as Mahatma Gandhi said, once we "turn the spotlight inward."

Why is objectivity a virtue?

In many ways this journey inward is dependent upon our ability simply to accept the reality of a situation. This is not the same as agreeing with what we see or liking it or even understanding it. It merely means that we see what is there to be seen. Accepting eyes are objective eyes, and objective eyes accept what they see, what is there, not what they want to see or what they wish were there.

The reason that objectivity is a virtue (certainly the most demanding yet clearly the beginning of all personal virtues) is that it is essential that we learn to be objective about the very things that normally define subjectivity—our thoughts and emotions. We must set aside our subjective selves to go in search of our true Selves. If we cannot take this first step, we cannot take the pilgrimage. Yet to be able to separate the ego-self from the greater Self, to see past our own emotions, thoughts, and behaviors initially (and theoretically) sounds impossible. How can we move beyond our personal involvement with ourselves—the very essence of subjectivity?

One way to do so is to consider the cardinal virtue of prudence. Its relationship to objectivity can be found in its meanings—deliberation, consideration, discretion, and discrimination—for the virtue of objectivity requires these same qualities. Unfortunately we have very little training in (and even fewer role models for) being either objective or prudent. Prudence is no longer in fashion; objectivity has become a rare phenomenon, even by those whose positions or roles require it. As a nation we are no longer shocked by biased judges or investigators, impulsive and indiscreet leaders, subjective juries, and opinionated and overly emotional media.

How many of us can admit that we do not know the "truth" when presented with the latest political scandal? How many of us take the time to deliberate both sides of a religious conflict? It seems that we are constantly being bombarded with controversial issues and expected to have strong and emotionally based opinions. And, if we have difficulty being objective with external realities, it is easy to see how much more difficult it is to be objective with an internal one.

To understand why objectivity is a virtue, try to imagine yourself saying, "I don't know the truth," the next time you don't know it. Picture yourself taking the time to deliberate, to gather relevant information, and to render an opinion based on fairness and awareness rather than convenience or tradition or comfort. In short, try to be an objective judge and understand all sides equally and fairly. The difficulty that you will encounter reflects the power and size of your own weak ego.

What is wrong with being subjective?

We have been trained to cherish our subjectivity and to place great weight on what we believe, think, feel, and value. We have learned that these very things distinguish us from others and make us unique. After all, our experiences and reactions to our own lives define us and give us a sense of self. We rely on our thoughts and feelings to help us know that we exist, that we are here and real and involved. We become attached to our perceptions and beliefs because they help structure our world and give us meaning. It is natural and comfortable to perceive ourselves through our thoughts and feelings; they enable us to make sense of our lives and of what we do.

One definition of *subjectivity* is something derived from the limitations of the mind rather than from reality independent of the mind. There is an even simpler way to describe this: a romantic. As novelist Anne Rivers Siddons aptly states, "A romantic refuses to look at things as they are, and that's the most dangerous thing in the world." For whatever the reasons and no matter how good the intentions, the romantic is first and foremost completely subjective. He has narrowed and limited reality to fit his idealistic construction of it or what he believes it "should" be. In order to sustain this fantasy, he will inevitably try to change the world so that it will conform to his perceptions. When reality does not acquiesce to his demands, the romantic becomes self-destructive, self-centered, frustrated, hopeless, and alone. His subjective ego ("what I want, what I need, what I believe") has consumed him, and all contact with objective reality is lost. Examples of the danger of being an extreme romantic abound: in literature, Lord Byron; in politics, former President Nixon; in business, John DeLorean; in the entertainment industry, Marilyn Monroe; in religion, Jim Jones. Because of our conditioning, there may be more romantics in this culture than there are realists.

Yet we like being subjective; we have spent years learning to judge the world from our perceptions of how it "should" be. Being objective, on the other hand, means that we must move beyond what we want and realistically see what is there. Not only is this very difficult to do, but it can be extremely frightening. For this involves leaving behind the things that we have created to help us feel safe and secure; we have to give up our defenses, illusions, expectations, and beliefs—the very things that we believe define us. It means leaving a comfortable place or, at least, a familiar place to go to one that is unknown. Why, we'd have to be out of our minds (literally!) to want to give up our subjective selves and become objective. And that is precisely why this journey is a pilgrimage.

How can I objectively define myself?

"Who am I?" you ask, and the answers you give reflect the limitations of the ego. "I am me. I am not you. I am different. I am what I do, the roles I play: mother, writer, psychologist, wife, daughter." The answers you give manifest your "me-ness," your uniqueness, that which differentiates you from others and identifies and defines you both to yourself and to the world. Your roles reflect your ego because they limit you only to what you do rather than expand you to who you really are. The ego also manifests in your needs to be loved and valued by others. You have learned that this is where you find your worth. It is no wonder that you tend to think that ego and self are one and the same. For if I am not my ego, then who in the world am I?

Perhaps the more relevant and objective question is "What am I?" The Buddha answered, "I am awake." Since we are not the Buddha, maybe it is enough to be content with "I am alive and I am aware." These answers, along with "I am human yet also made in the image of God," transport you to a Self much larger than your ego. They take you to another level of you, a deeper level of being that is unlimited and part of the Whole. They allow you to discover that there is more to you than meets the eye or is demonstrated by your mind and body. You are more than you can see, greater than what you think or feel. You possess an innate reality that defines you and connects you to a greater reality that completes you; this internal reality is your soul.

What is the weak ego?

The differentiation between the ego-self and the larger Self is a lifelong process of first becoming involved and then learning to detach from our involvements. We simply cannot experience this larger Self—the objective, detached Self—without first going through the ego—the subjective, attached self. In the beginning we mirror who we are through the eyes of others. Because we all are born helpless and completely dependent upon others for survival and identity, attachment is necessary. We need others in order to exist, and so we attach to them and depend on them. The development of the ego represents a necessary separation of the individual infant from the mother or primary caretaker: "I am not her; I am me."

When we are very young, we need to be both separate and attached; we need both in order to develop. As we mature, we equate our separation with individuality and our attachments with security. Thus, we remain attached long after we need to do so in order to survive. We remain attached to others because it is familiar and it gives us an illusion of safety. By the time we become young adults, we discover that we are caught in the dilemma of wanting to be both separate (individual) and attached (intimate). Our attachments have become both our identities and our prisons.

The things that we are attached to often become more important than our individual selves ("Everything I do is for you"); even worse, our attachments quickly become what we use to determine our worth ("If I do this, you will think I'm good"). Whenever we externalize our identities (define ourselves through others or our status, fame, wealth, or possessions), we severely limit or even entirely lose our internal selves. Thus, whenever we perceive ourselves as only egos, we sever the connection to our souls. In the process we develop the weak ego.

Because all others and all things outside ourselves are not within our control (we can lose them at any time), this ego-self is weak—vulnerable, dependent, limiting, and totally subjective. In order to feel powerful and strong, it causes us to become egocentric, to see the world only through our limited and dependent eyes, our unfulfilled needs, and our numerous wants. Whatever happens is only as relevant as it affects us; whatever we feel or desire becomes the critical issue of the moment, the reality of our world.

Why is the weak ego a problem?
Living in the weak ego is not strange or unusual; we often feel comfortable in this state because it is so common. Perhaps it is initially even constructive and beneficial: We

have to be attached before we can detach; we have to have something before we can lose it. Moreover, we can easily relate to others because they are also driven and consumed by their own weak egos. Insecurity is rampant; it is the core of most communications, relationships, interactions, and cultures. We develop facades to hide and deny our insecurities; we try to fool the world into perceiving us, not as what we fear we are (helpless and vulnerable) but as what we think we should be (strong and knowing). If we are very good at it and develop strong weak egos (this is not a contradiction of terms but unfortunately a common occurrence), sometimes we even manage to fool ourselves. This usually requires strong, successful attachments to the externals: power over others, fame, money, status, recognition, and worldly achievement.

The weak ego is a hard taskmaster; it is never satisfied and does not know the meaning of *enough*. It is voraciously hungry and continually consuming whatever it is given. Like any other addiction, it quickly becomes a bottomless pit that can never be filled. It is exactly because of this insatiability that we ultimately tire of the effort to gratify it and begin to search for something else to fulfill us. Eventually, unless we remain extremely stubborn (a sure sign of ego), we become unable to continue the work involved in maintaining the facade, defending against our insecurities, and deriving our worth from others who are often more insecure than we are. It is then, when we are exhausted and frustrated, that we let down our guards—

our defenses—and become confused, afraid, and ready for change. It is then that we become open to the discovery that we are more than our egos and that what we really want and need is not to be found in the externals of life, no matter how seductive they are.

What is the process?

A good answer to this is found in the Hindu religion, which delineates the four basic human wants: (1) pleasure, (2) worldly success (fame, power, and wealth), (3) duty (to give, to be of service), and (4) infinite being, infinite knowledge, and infinite joy. The first two wants represent the Path of Desire, which is a subjective but necessary stage of life. Therefore, it is natural for us to believe initially that personal desires are the most critical ones. The child desires pleasure, the young adult desires recognition and worldly success, and during the middle stage of life (the thirties and forties), it is normal to desire fame, status, power, and money. When we choose the Path of Desire, we can go after it without guilt or negativity, according to Hindu thought, because we need to attach to these external desires so that we may later detach from them. Eventually we learn that the Path of Desire is only an illusion of happiness created by the subjective and limited weak ego; it cannot satisfy what we really want. This brings us to the next path.

The final two wants represent the Path of Renunciation. Typically, once we arrive at the discovery that external wants do not satisfy us (we renounce the Path of Desire), we turn to duty: our needs to be of service, to be of use to others. The wish to gain has been replaced by the wish to give. This is the beginning of the Path of Renunciation. This path satisfies our wants for external praise and internal self-respect, but because it involves others in order to feel worthy, it still does not satisfy our internal quest for meaning. Surprisingly, because this is not what we are taught, the path of duty is still in the domain of the weak ego.

All external desires are ultimately unfulfilling; they are limited (finite) and imperfect. It is only the fourth want—infinite being, infinite knowledge, infinite joy—that leads to true fulfillment, but in order to arrive at this realization, we must move past the ego and our dependence on the external world. We can either detach from the finite self or attach to infinite reality; both are the same phenomenon. Paradoxically, when we do, we discover that we already have everything we want; it is inside us.

When will I begin?
In order to realize your being, your awareness, and your joy, the only path to true fulfillment, you must move beyond your subjective self, the ego, and discover your objective inner Self. There is no other way to discover the fourth path. The process of learning to be objective is not quick or easy; it goes against everything you have already learned. It is frightening because you must do it alone; it is

unfamiliar and uncertain because you must leave behind your illusions of security, success, and power. But in order to be real, to be actualized, alive, and aware, you have no other choice. The purpose for becoming subjective—developing the weak ego—was to form your identity, allay your fears, create an illusion of control, and feel secure. You were taught to rely on your perceptions and emotions to help you identify who you really are, and when your reality conflicted with someone else's creation of reality, you learned to dismiss or deny the other and return to your familiar way of being. Thus, the very nature of what you have learned to define as reality was subjective.

As you mature, it becomes more and more difficult to rely on your perception of reality to keep you safe and comfortable. There comes a time when the cost of maintaining your defenses and your personal construction of the world exceeds the rewards from doing so. The cost of remaining subjective is much too high and utilizes all your energy and time. This is when the extent of your own insecurities becomes evident, both to yourself and to others, and the effort required to maintain a facade of security becomes overwhelming. Subjectivity creates pathology because it is not realistic to be aware of only your own existence, your own needs and feelings, desires, and beliefs. Living in reality means recognizing that you are only one of the multitude and that everyone else has his own needs and wants.

And yet you are much more than just one of many. Inside you is the desire to be; you want to be alive, to know; you want to be aware and to feel joy; you want to be free from boredom, frustration, laziness, and pain. In trying to satisfy these essential human needs, you may already have discovered that the externals of life do not fulfill your interior life. You may already have traveled the Path of Desire and found yourself still empty and hungry. Perhaps you have tried the way of duty and also recognize its limitations. If you, like most of us, are still attached to external fulfillment, you are probably confused because nothing you have is enough. Your subjective thinking has caused you to perceive yourself as one ego among many egos; becoming objective will set you free.

This discovery—the start of your pilgrimage—can also be called the desert experience because as soon as you let go of your attachments to the externals, you enter strange country. This place is lonely, barren, arid, and often boring, for you are no longer attached to the normal stimulations; they no longer work for you. You have not traveled long enough to discover the oasis inside you, so you seem to be stuck in a "no-man's-land." You need to journey through this terrible place; you need to have faith and keep going even though the terrain is unfamiliar and you are terrified. Remember that every prophet, every wise and holy being, has had this desert experience before he found what he was seeking. The soul lives in the deepest, darkest recesses within you, yet it is here where the light is discovered. Think of this part of your journey as a tunnel and know that the light is at the end.

How can I become infinite?

When the weak ego is very large and powerful (when you judge your worth only from externals), the true Self becomes suppressed inside the ego. Then your being is limited by your doing; your knowledge is limited by ignorance; your joy is limited by physical pain and frustration because of unmet desires and boredom with life. When you are consumed by the weak ego, these limitations define and overwhelm you. But when you move beyond the limitations of the ego, when you identify your self with all being, your own being becomes unlimited. The noted philosopher and professor of religion Huston Smith makes this very clear: "Each desire that aims at the ego's gratification adds a grain to the wall that surrounds the individual self and insulates it from the infinite sea of being that surrounds it, whereas each impulse towards participation in that larger life dislodges a grain from the cramping dike." As soon as you recognize your inherent goodness and begin to love and esteem yourself and discover that what you truly desire is to move beyond your limitations, to become infinite, the egoless Self develops. Then you become alive, aware, and actualized. Then you become virtuous in yourself and for yourself.

When do you begin? You begin when you realize that

you are on a never-ending treadmill, that you are doing more and more, working harder and harder, going faster and faster for rewards that mean less and less. You begin when you understand Aldous Huxley when he said, "There comes a time when one asks even of Shakespeare, even of Beethoven, is this all?" You begin when that old Peggy Lee song "Is That All There Is?" begins to sound like your song.

How do you begin? You begin by detaching from the power of your mind. You begin by recognizing that science, philosophy, and logic deal with reason and that reason is limited by the experience you have to work with. Spiritual truths are not logical or even verbal; they do not come from reason. They precede reason and are personal and intuitive. Therefore, you need to set reason—your active and noisy mind—aside. As Confucianists say, "To the mind that is still, the universe surrenders."

How can I practice objectivity?

Objective eyes are egoless; they see reality without judgment or limitations. Objective hearts are open; they feel unlimited and unconditional love. The soul is already objective; it is not interested in worldly pleasure or external gratifications or even duty toward others. In order to become aware of your own soul, you simply must subdue the weak ego. Its voice is loud, clamoring, boisterous, and incessant; the voice of your soul is soft, quiet, and not often heard. Therefore, it is impossible to know your soul unless your mind (controlled by the weak ego) is still, your heart open, and your focus turned inward.

Perhaps the easiest way to practice objectivity is to recognize that you are more than what you previously thought you were. You are greater than you know, better than you hope, and you are able to realize your potential for connection and belongingness. What has stopped this recognition is your limited and weak ego, your involvement with and attachment to others. The price you have paid for ego gratification has cost you your involvement with the Whole and your connection to your soul. You do not have to continue to pay such a high price. Take the biggest risk of your life: Let go. Detach your Self from your weak ego. Change your focus for fulfillment from the externals to your internal being. Instead of identifying yourself as who you are, begin to think in terms of what you are.

How do I constrain my ego?

The process of differentiating the ego from the self is the beginning of the concept of religion. As theologian Huston Smith states, ". . . true religion begins with the quest for meaning and value beyond privacy—with renunciation of the ego's claims to finality." All religions deal with this quest. Perhaps this need to renounce the weak ego is demonstrated most graphically by the Hindu statue of the dancing god Shiva; his left foot is raised in the air while his right foot is planted firmly on a dwarf representing the human ego, that noisy, spoiled aspect of ourselves that demands to have its own way. This depiction clearly and simply shows that only when the ego is constrained can we experience the power of our true nature and understand our connection to a greater reality.

Like the statue of Shiva, plant your foot firmly upon your weak ego. Begin by recognizing that you have a weak ego—we all do—and that it is not all of you or the best of you. Part of the weak ego is manifested by that negative voice, the critic's voice, that always tells you what you are doing wrong. Stop listening to this voice as if it were real or important. This is not your conscience talking, for your conscience tells you that you have done something bad but that you yourself are good. The voice of the weak ego tells you that you are bad and that what you have done proves it. Your weak ego also manifests itself whenever you judge your worth from something external to you. It is operating when you perceive your value through the eyes of someone else. It is also in control whenever you perceive the world through your own limitations or unfulfilled needs—your subjective eyes or desires.

The weak ego is always seeking love and approval from external sources. Therefore, the best way to subdue or control it is to love yourself. Love yourself unconditionally, just as you are right now. This requires realistically accepting your limitations, your frailties and imperfections, the present state of your human condition. The weak ego feeds your insecurities while trying to hide these same insecurities from others; ironically, it creates what it then tries to deny. Remember, its goal is to impress others at the expense of knowing the true Self. Therefore, nothing else will constrain the weak ego as surely and as quickly as accepting and loving your imperfect self. In order to do so, you will have to stop trying to be or appearing to be perfect. Also, you will need to become aware of your own dark side. The weak ego works hard to deny or hide this dark side, consisting of your weaknesses and all too human fears. It is in your dark side that your true Self is buried; it is in the denial of this dark side that your ego is nurtured.

Author and therapist Thomas Moore says that the soul also lives in the shadow side. Therefore, when you deny the dark side of yourself, you are actually denying the soul—your very connection to God, the goodness within you. Your journey to your soul is a journey through your internal Self. It is a quest to live your goodness and to realize your potential: to be fully and completely human and to know that you are an image of God. Your physical life must begin with attachment to externals, but your spiritual life begins with detachment from them. You begin this detachment process as soon as you start becoming objective about the nature of your true Self.

What does detachment feel like?
When I die, I know that I will have to let go, to detach from everything that is familiar to me except my soul. At

fifty I can already tell that this detachment process has begun. So many things just do not seem that important to me anymore. I look with wonder on my grown daughters, now in their twenties, and remember how serious my life seemed at their age, how intense and how dramatic. I do not seem to have much drama anymore, and I love my solitude and peace. Nothing is as clear to me as it is to them; nothing requires that much energy. But I remember, and I wonder what has happened to get me from there to here. The biggest change is that I am slowly (painfully slowly) becoming more accepting of how things are; I am more reconciled to the fact that I can change so very little and that what I can change or control is not out there in the world but right here in me.

I empathize with their involvements, their passions, and their pains, but I do not want to be twenty or thirty or even forty again. I now recognize that I could not detach from the externals until I was first intensely attached to them, and I am glad that I lived each previous decade passionately. I look back and laugh at my certainty, my righteousness, my ability to know so strongly and to preach what I knew so vociferously. Now I understand why I was "a pain in the ass, but an interesting one," as a friend once told me. I still have my moments, but more and more I catch myself and admit that I am not as sure as I sound, not nearly as convinced as I pretend to be. I am beginning to be objective; I understand the value of acceptance. And one day I believe that I will be able to detach even from this differentiation between acceptance and rejection. As the Buddhists believe, then I will transcend the opposites and understand "that which is sin is also wisdom." I now recognize that the virtue of objectivity is that it leads to a reconciliation of opposites, that this is the path to the "stillness inside of the dance."

How do I become more objective?

When I interned at the Veterans Administration Medical Center in Houston, my mentor, Buzz O'Connell, used to conduct the following exercise during group therapy. Perhaps it will help you separate from your weak ego and discover the deeper aspects of yourself; I know it helped me. Buzz placed three chairs in the middle of the room in a small circle facing one another. One chair he labeled the "weak ego," another the "observing I," and the third was the "deep self" (the soul).

All three roles represented three aspects of one person. Three volunteers from the group played the roles specified by the chairs, understanding that they were playing parts of the person in the weak ego chair. This participant had the easiest role because he would sit and talk pretty much as usual. "I am so dumb. Look at all the mistakes I have made in my life. I screw up everything I touch. Everyone else is better than me. I don't deserve to be loved because I'm such a failure." And so on.

The observing I always had the hardest job (there is no training for this role; you learn it by experiencing it), and

Buzz would help. The role called for neutral and realistic comments to the weak ego's litany. It also called for encouragement. "It is interesting you say that, but is that always true? Yes, but look at all the things you have done right. Look at what you have learned. Aren't you doing the best you can under the circumstances? Of course you deserve to be loved. You are good. I love you. You cannot be perfect, so you are not a perfect failure. Why are you so hard on yourself? Give yourself a break. Laugh at yourself; why are you always so serious?" And so on.

Initially the volunteer playing the deep self role rarely had much to say. (After all, the soul will not communicate when the mind and ego are babbling away.) Once in a while, when the observing I made a point that stopped the weak ego, the deep self would say, "Yes" or "Good" or "That's right!" Sometimes it would say, "I care" or "I love you," and this was incredibly powerful. Because this voice could be heard only when the weak ego was silent, as the observing I became more certain and powerful and listened to, the deep self had more opportunities to be heard. Often, after the exercise was over, the participant playing the deep self commented that it needed the observing I in order to be noticed at all. Without it the weak ego ran the show. When the observing I became very strong and confident, the weak ego voice often became quite funny and sometimes even ludicrous.

What we all learned from this exercise was that the observing I is the connection to the deep self. It is the simplest and shortest way to subdue the noisy and discouraging weak ego in order to become aware of that quiet but powerful soul. The attachment to the weak ego causes the loss of attachment to the inner self. Becoming objective means detaching from the externals in order to discover the internal self. You can use this exercise upon yourself, and you don't even need the chairs! Next time your weak ego voice starts becoming overwhelming, practice your noncritical, nonjudging, encouraging observing I voice. And listen objectively for your deep self. Eventually you will hear it.

What is the lesson? A teaching story

I will end each of the chapters of this book with an ancient teaching story that exemplifies the virtue being discussed. Of all the teaching stories that I know and tell, this first one is the most difficult. Even though I frequently told it in therapy sessions or in self-development workshops, it haunted me. Initially I took this story literally and had a hard time dealing with its message. When I first heard it fifteen years ago, I did not understand that everything we have, own, or love is a gift and is temporary. Then I did not want to know as much about acceptance and letting go as this story teaches. Now I am beginning to understand that this story is about becoming objective. While its literal meaning may seem painfully impossible, its higher meaning is essential.

This story is not about the inability to love or become

involved or committed; rather, it is about becoming involved, loving deeply, and still being able to accept the reality of the situation even though it may not be what we want. This story is about letting go with love, which may be the most difficult of all of life's tasks. The ability first to accept lovingly and later to detach lovingly is always going to be extremely painful, but this is the reality behind the virtue of objectivity.

LONG AGO IN a far-off land there was a small fishing village where lived a beautiful young woman. One day she gave birth to a child, even though she was not married. All the fishermen gathered together and went to her humble home to discover who was the father of her son. After much time and coercion from the group of angry fishermen, the young mother reluctantly admitted that the father of her infant son was the monk who lived in solitary isolation in the small monastery on the hill above the village. Upon learning this, the fishermen talked among themselves and decided that the only right thing to do was to take the baby to its father. That very night, they lit their torches, grabbed the boy away from his mother, climbed up the steep hill, and knocked on the monastery door. It was very late, and it took some time for the monk to answer. It was obvious when he opened the door that he had been rudely awakened. The fishermen explained why they were there and thrust the infant at the monk. His only reply, upon taking the child and closing the door, was "Ah so."

Eight years passed. The beautiful young mother became critically ill and called the fishermen together at her deathbed. She told them that she had lied about the father of her child and that indeed the true father was one of the married fishermen. Again the fishermen talked among themselves and decided to remedy their injustice. Again they lit their torches and climbed up the mountain to the monastery. Yet again they knocked on the door and awoke the sleeping monk. But this time, when he opened the door, they saw an adorable young boy peeking out from behind the monk's robes. There was obviously great love between the old monk and the young child. The fishermen explained the situation, apologized for their error, and grabbed the young boy away from the monk. As the monk closed the door, they again heard him say, "Ah so."

The degree to which I love myself
is the degree to which I have integrity.

2

THE SECOND STEP:
Integrity

THE TRUNK WAS large, old, and very ugly. It was so ugly that my daughter Jennifer could not understand why I was interested in it. We were shopping, as we often did, for bargains in out-of-the-way junk shops and places that call their wares antiques but are in reality castoffs. I love such places because there is always the possibility of a find, something wonderful for very little money. I thought this trunk had that potential.

The problem with the trunk was that it had been painted a hot, lurid, bright pink. All of it was pink: the metal, the wood, the fastenings, even the fancy trim work. Someone had taken the easy way and simply spray-painted the entire thing this hideous pink. Jennifer saw the pink and was revolted; I saw the potential and was interested. Underneath that all-invasive paint was a trunk in good condition. There was no rust or water damage, and the fittings were intact, except for the leather handles, which were easily replaceable. The trunk looked pathetic, and it called out to me. The fifty-dollar price—"today only"—made up my mind. Before the owner could change her mind, I bought it, loaded it into the backseat of the car (no easy feat given its size), and took it home. I experienced the thrill of the "find"; Jennifer remained dubious.

Redoing this trunk was more work than I had antici-pated. What I had not realized was that the pink paint was lead-based; therefore, it had been there a long time. Modern paint removers are not very effective on old paint, paint that has seeped into wood fibers and bonded with metal. I also could not know that underneath the pink were layers of blue, white, yellow, and black paint. This trunk had been around awhile and in many different disguises. For three weeks I scraped and sanded and lived amid paint remover fumes. My hands were a wreck, my fingernails decimated, my eyes seemed permanently red and swollen. But the longer I worked on it, the more determined I became. I was going to get that trunk back to its original state.

At first the trunk seemed to resist my efforts. But after a while it actually seemed to participate in its rebirth. And one day, the day that I removed the last of the paints and old varnish, it actually seemed to breathe. I looked at the trunk, and it was bigger and more beautiful than I had ever imagined. Somehow, it looked free and happy and glorious, just from being stripped and relieved of its many facades. In its natural state it had integrity.

The concept of integrity haunted me from that day forward. Everything that I did to that trunk, from the lightest coating of paint, to the stain on the wood, to the leather handles, to the final protective topcoat, was influenced and guided by the trunk's innate integrity. True, it was not perfect—it had gouged scars, scratches, and dents that could never be corrected—but these added, rather than detracted, from its character. After all, this trunk was old, and it wore its memories and experiences; I did not want it to appear new and pristine. I valued it for its age, and this was what had given it its integrity—its meaning and its worth.

What is integrity?

As I was working on the trunk, I realized how parallel this experience was to what I do as a therapist. I recognized that the process of therapy involves stripping away the facades until the true Self, the self beyond the ego, can be observed and heard. All life, all our worldly experiences, contribute to who we become. When we use our lives to develop our facades—our appearances rather than our realities—we become similar to that many-layered trunk. After a time these many layers of experience begin to inhibit our underlying realities. Like the trunk, we lose our underlying selves; we find we cannot breathe, and we no longer know who we are in there under all those disguises.

Finding the true Self—the connection to the innermost being—always involves stripping and chipping away at the external presentation, whether done with the help of a therapist or by ourselves. It always involves hard work and requires determination and the willingness to feel pain and vulnerability. Discovering our integrity is not an easy or quick process. Just as it takes many years to erect the facades that hide us from our true Selves, it also takes time to recognize and dissemble these external layers. It is no wonder that this is viewed as a formidable task; it is not surprising that we usually believe that it is easier to keep the facades and continue, as best we can, living only in an external reality. Our egos, nurtured by our insecurities, keep us imprisoned in our facades; the more we add to our external layers, the farther we get from our inner natures, our integrity.

Why is integrity a virtue?
Integrity is defined as "the quality of being complete or whole." It is manifested through our characters, our sincerity, honesty, experience, totality and entirety of ourselves. More simply perhaps, it represents the being of the true Self. It requires the recognition of our innate goodness and our willingness to live that goodness. Surely, it is one of the most difficult of virtues. For having integrity is another way of saying that we do justice to our Selves, that we live and serve our souls completely and without reservation. We do not usually equate the cardinal virtue of justice to ourselves; we rarely think of it as something we do for our Selves, but this is indeed the essence of integrity. The medieval mystic Julian of Norwich explained the relationship between these two virtues. "Justice is that thing which is so good it cannot be better than it is." Another early mystic, Meister Eckhart, also addressed this: "If a man is in justice, he is in God and he is God."

Integrity, then, requires that we recognize and acknowledge that we are more than what we think we are: Inside us exists the ultimate goodness. This goodness exists as an integral and defining part of who we are. It comes from a power greater than we can know, a power that exists both separate from us and intimately connected to us. We cannot become good; we cannot work toward this state. It has been given to us; our challenge is first to recognize and then to live this goodness, to make it manifest in every moment of our lives. For this is what integrity entails.

What is one path to integrity?

Lao-tzu, the creator of Taoism, became disenchanted and saddened by his countrymen's lack of interest in realizing and cultivating their natural goodness. One day he quietly left China for Tibet, but before he was allowed to leave, he was asked to write down his beliefs. This he did, and his one tiny book is the heart of the Taoist religion. His concept of Tao can be interpreted as three different things. Tao means the way of ultimate reality or the meaning of existence, which man can never know in this life; this definition is transcendent and experienced only through mystical insight. Tao also means the way of the universe, the power of nature, and the integration of the whole; thus, it is immanent and demonstrated throughout all nature. The third meaning, however, is the most relevant for understanding integrity: Tao is the way man can live his life in order to relate and conform to nature and the ultimate reality.

"The way to do," according to Lao-tzu, "is to be." Thus, in order to be, we must move beyond our doing. "When our private egos and conscious efforts yield to a power not their own," as author and theologian Huston Smith interprets Tao, we discover a simplicity and a freedom that flow, not from us, but through us. When we get the foundation of the Self in harmony with Tao, our behavior will be natural and correct. Then our doing will follow our being.

What this means is that we cannot separate our integrity (our being) into isolated incidents or behaviors. We cannot say we have integrity because once we did not lie or cheat. In order to have integrity, we must recognize our inner natures and continually be true to these deeper Selves. Everything we do, everything we are, every thought we entertain determine our characters, our very beings, our integrity. This requires the balance between our wisdom (awareness) and our method (practice). The foundation for the true Self is based on this interrelationship; who we really are is composed of both what we know and how we act. Integrity, then, is the manifestation of this balance.

What is the nature of perfect balance?
Buddha exemplified the perfect balance between awareness and practice. His life is a testament to the virtue of

integrity. Buddha was not a god but a human who managed to attain enlightenment in his life. He was born in India around 560 B.C. as a wealthy prince, but he renounced all worldly goods in his twenties and spent six years searching for meaning or enlightenment. Having achieved it through heroic experiences, he spent the next half century preaching what he had discovered. The essence of his philosophy is contained in the Four Noble Truths and the Eightfold Path.

Briefly, Buddha's Four Noble Truths are: (1) Life is suffering (misery is at the core of human life); (2) the misery comes from our desires to fulfill our egos (satisfying the ego limits and insulates us from the Universal Whole); (3) the cure to our suffering is found in our release from self-interest (we become free when we move past the boundaries of the ego); and (4) the way to release ourselves is through the Eightfold Path.

In other words, Buddha discovered that the true nature of man, the image of God within man, is hidden underneath the ego—the desire for self-interest and meaning derived from external sources. The ego creates the facade of self-importance, which separates us from others but, even more important, separates us from our inner Selves, our true natures. When the ego is in control or unconstrained, we are similar to a lamp covered by dust; the light is faint and can no longer shine through. We are also like the trunk covered by layers of paint obliterating our true beauty. The ego causes us to keep adding more dust or paint, further separating us from our inner natures and our integrity.

How can I discover my own true nature?

Buddha's answer to living our true natures consists of eight conditions or practices; these are closely related to the doctrines found in all religions. However, he has been compared with a modern therapist because he used a psychological rather than a spiritual approach to solve the problems of life. Buddha's approach is based on first observation, then diagnosis, and finally treatment. The Eightfold Path, according to Professor Huston Smith, "is not external treatment passively accepted by the patient as coming from without; it is not treatment by pills or cult or grace. It is treatment by training . . . treatment by practice." Buddha's eight treatment steps are preceded by the concept of right association, or the need to find a teacher or an appropriate role model. Again this is consistent with the comparison of this approach with psychotherapy.

The Eightfold Path consists of: right knowledge (being aware of the Four Noble Truths), right aspiration (the consistent intention to transcend our separateness), right speech (telling the truth and speaking charitably), right behavior (avoidance of killing, stealing, lying, being unchaste or intoxicated), right livelihood (engaging in occupations that encourage life and do not destroy it and realizing that work is not the ultimate end but the means to life), right effort (developing virtues, curbing passions, and transcending evil through will), right mindfulness (always being alert and examining the self), and right absorption (finding harmony among the body, mind, and spirit by consciously going within).

It is readily observable that Buddha's answers to finding and living our true natures cover every aspect of our beings. They integrate all facets of ourselves and demonstrate the strong and important relationships between what we think, say, act, believe and do with who we are and what we become. This path is a process, not a state, and requires a lifetime of practice. Knowing what to do, like insight, is not the answer; it is just the beginning of the awareness. The real work is in the practice, the experience of doing that leads to the being. This concept brings us full circle: Tao says the way to do is to be; Buddha suggests that the way to be is to do. Maybe Frank Sinatra captured the circle when he crooned "Do be do be do." In reality, our doing and our being cannot be separated, just as integrity cannot be separated from the true Self.

Why is honesty critical to integrity?
In two of Buddha's eight approaches toward enlightenment, the importance of being truthful is stressed. Buddha believed that deceit is negative because it reduces the liar's being; lying occurs because of the fear of revealing the true Self. There seems to be a clear correlation between being deceitful and being insecure; deception usually involves protection of the ego. Nowhere is this more evident than

in our relationships with our inner Selves. While being honest is clearly a critical aspect of having integrity, the importance of this quality, perhaps contrary to our training, is not what we do and say to others but that we are brutally honest with ourselves. And this is a far more difficult task.

The ego develops from our needs for attachment and approval; in the beginning of our lives it is a necessary and normal creation of our individuality. We need to separate from others in order to individuate, and this is what the development of the ego produces: a sense that each of us is significant and different. In order to maintain this perception of ourselves, we utilize defenses, create illusions, and develop senses of self-importance. As we become more familiar with our creations, we forget that they are self-made realities and not part of the greater reality. The ego deludes us into feeling secure inside the facades that it constructs. We become "me" as separate from "you." These distinctions give us a perception of uniqueness; they create an illusion of safety. But what we have created in order to protect ourselves—our ego boundaries—are also boundaries that separate us from our inner Selves. They become our personal prisons; while their original purpose was to keep the world at bay, all too soon they keep us away from our connection to the greater and more meaningful reality.

In its never-ending quest for self-importance and satisfaction, the ego detaches from anything unifying and connective. To protect itself, it will eventually cause us to detach from all humanity and, even worse, from our innate goodness, our spirits and souls, and even our thoughts, feelings, and physical bodies. When we allow the ego to control the mind and to tell us what we want and need (in other words, to externalize our worth), we quickly disassociate from our internal being. The ego is a natural dictator that will brook no interference and share no power or control, even with the other aspects of ourselves. Like many dictators, upon tasting power, it quickly becomes a megalomaniac. For once it discovers that it is easier to create illusions of power and control than it is to develop real power, it becomes a formidable adversary to the true Self. In order to protect the illusion of its own power, it must use deceit. Thus, our own egos become our own worst enemies, and constraining the ego becomes our most challenging task.

Stopping the ego is therefore critical for discovering the soul. This is very difficult, for first we must distinguish between the true Self, which is connected to the soul, and the false self of worldly experience, the ego. When we believe that the ego is more powerful than the Self, we have no escape. The German mystic Meister Eckhart revealed that the only way to dissolve the boundaries of the self is to reach beyond the frailty of the ego: "It is always you yourself that hinders yourself. . . . Therefore, begin first with yourself and forsake yourself. Truly you will then flee first from yourself, whatever else you may flee." The self he is referring to is of course the ego-self. There is no room for deceit in this difficult process; total honesty with our true Selves is the only way we can subdue the ego and live with integrity.

What is impeccability?

Another way to approach this virtue is to understand the concept of *impeccability,* which means being without sin, error, or defect. Because we are human and therefore imperfect, we can never completely attain this, but we can strive toward it. One of the best descriptions of this striving is found in Carlos Castaneda's eight books detailing his experiences with the old Yaqui Indian don Juan. What don Juan, a sorcerer and a man of great knowledge, tried to teach Castaneda was the way of the warrior: ". . . a warrior is impeccable when he trusts his personal power, regardless of whether it is small or enormous." Don Juan tells Castaneda that the journey to knowledge is similar to going to war; it is approached with awareness, respect, fear, yet also absolute confidence.

The journey to the soul, our highest form of self-knowledge, causes us to become warriors because we must fight against our insecurities, weaknesses, and limitations—in short, the domain of the ego. Author Victor Sanchez states that don Juan's "way of the warrior is a myth of our time," for it serves the function of all myths "to reflect our most worthy and dignified aspirations as mortals, inviting us to turn them into reality." Sanchez paraphrases don Juan: "The way of the warrior is a form of constantly living the challenge of being . . . Perhaps the most telling characteristic of a warrior is the perennial search for impeccability in every action, even the smallest. The warrior understands impeccability as giving the best in everything he or she does, which implies making optimum use of individual energy. Even when all other motivations crumble, the warrior will persist in acting impeccably, if just for the sake of impeccability alone."

How can I become impeccable?

Castaneda's eight books form a remarkable tale of one man's journey toward integrity. Don Juan reveals nothing directly or concisely, yet in a very simple way he teaches the constrainment of the ego. The warrior begins by moving past the rational or the power of the mind controlled by the ego in order to attend to feelings and discover personal power. This requires freeing the self from attachments and needs and recognizing that death is imminent. When this is done, every moment becomes important and energy is expended on taking control over the self and the personal world. This control is critical.

Therefore, having integrity means that we take control over what we can control. And if we control it, we are responsible for it. In reality we completely control only two things: the way we feel about ourselves and our behaviors based on our feelings. We do not control our feelings, but we do control the choice to feel good about ourselves (self-esteem) or feel bad about ourselves (weak ego). We do not control all our behaviors—snoring, sneezing, twitches, and tics, for example—but we do control our actions and reactions. We do not control fate, reality, the weather, timing, situation, or circumstance, but we do control what we do with them. Above all, we do not control others, no matter how much we want to. But we do control what we say, think, do, and ultimately feel about all others. Impeccability then means taking control of what we can control; integrity means actively living that responsibility.

What is the monkey mind?

Because of our training and experience and because of a lifetime of habit, our minds tend to listen to the voice of the ego and try to ignore that other unknown, scary, and less heard voice of the soul. Our minds are powerful; they tell us what we think, believe, and know and often even what we feel. More often than not our minds are controlled by the dictator we mentioned above, the ego. Our minds are so much a part of us, of our lives, that we rarely stop to question what they really are or to look objectively at what is going on in there. If we did, we might be surprised at how chaotic and uncontrolled our minds usually are.

Japanese Zen uses a phrase called the monkey mind, which is explained by Donald Richie. The phrase comes from an old sermon describing the mind of a human "as active, inquisitive, willful, and impatient as a monkey. It leaps from thought to thought, examining this curiosity or that, always losing interest and springing off again on some new and aimless quest." (Doesn't this sound just like the ego?) The purpose of this sermon is to show us that our uncontrolled minds often behave intolerably. Richie continues: "Few of us would choose a monkey as a lifetime companion, yet we all choose to live with our monkey minds. Thus, we are like unwilling owners of gibbons, forever straining at the leash—or of gorillas, who simply pick up a person and carry him along."

The question this sermon poses, one that is related to the concept of integrity, is this: If one lived with a real monkey, what would one do? The answer of course is to discipline it so that one's life could become endurable. So it is with our minds. In order to have self-control, to become an impeccable warrior, to have integrity, we must have control over our minds (and egos). The mind can be trained; it is part of us, and we know that we can be trained. The mind can be constrained; we have learned to constrain other aspects of ourselves—our behaviors, attitudes, and bodily functions—and we can also learn to control the mind.

The mind is like the ego; usually we prefer to be unconscious or unaware of both of them. It seems too much work to attend and become aware of them. Again from Richie: "We would not become aware of our minds if we could help it. Eventually, however, we cannot help it."

The training is simple, but it is not easy. Make the mind concentrate. Stop letting it fling itself about, and make it attend to one thing. Drag it back when it runs off; order it to stop when it is scampering around. Be patient and be firm. Give it something challenging to think about, and make it stay focused for an allotted period of time. Diligence and effort will pay off; over time the mind will become more quiet, and eventually it will become docile. "Finally, it will come when you call it and sit with you. Perhaps not for long, but for a time. When this occurs the monkey mind has finally become aware of itself. It has wakened. And to wake your mind is the first step toward wakening yourself."

How do I become integrated?

The way of the warrior is a good analogy for having integrity. As soon as you recognize that you are at war with yourself, you become a warrior. You have an ego pushing and enticing you toward the externals in life to give you worth and meaning, to find happiness and comfort. You probably like your ego; as you have grown older, you have become attached to it. You surely enjoy it when it is coddled and catered to—for a while, anyway. If you are like me, you like what is easy and familiar and produces some type of comfort and attention. After all, you have made some sense out of this chaotic world by constructing your facade, putting up your boundaries, and having a sense of self-importance. All this feels safe.

Yet sometimes don't you feel unconnected, out of balance, or even hopelessly lost? You probably have heard another voice, not frequently but enough to know it exists, that says there is something more, something better, something deeper than the superficial quest for pleasure and comfort. This voice is uncomfortable, unfamiliar, and unsure, but it has great power, and you are instinctively drawn to it. No wonder your ego hates it.

Your lifetime war has begun. Once you realize that there is more to you than your ego, you have entered the battle against your own ego. Once you become aware that you have a monkey mind and that your ego likes it to be unaware and undisciplined, you have begun the war to discipline your mind. And once you recognize that your integrity demands an integration of all parts of you in order to be manifested, your struggle to be honest with yourself has begun. Now that you have awareness, now that you are awake and desire an integration of yourself, how do you begin?

How do I practice integrity?

One way to begin the process of connection is paradoxical: Separate your voices. Becoming objective helped you see that you have different aspects of yourself: the weak ego, the objective I, and the deep self or soul. Now try the exercise of separating your ego voice from your self-esteeming or egoless voice. Imagine that you have a small dark imp on your right shoulder that talks to you in your right ear. This is your ego's voice, and you know it well; it has also been called the critic's voice. On your left shoulder, you have a lovely shining angel; this is your self-esteeming voice. It has also been called your guardian angel. From now on, whenever you hear a voice talking to you, put it on the appropriate shoulder and clearly label which voice is speaking.

In the beginning you probably will hear the imp's voice; this is because it is so powerful and familiar and used to being heard. Do not let this voice control what you hear. Pull up your angel voice so that you can have a fair fight. When the ego voice says something, allow the esteeming voice equal time. For example, the imp voice tells you that you are stupid because you made a mistake. Before you react or believe this voice, allow the angel voice its turn. You may have to help this voice out; it may not be used to being heard, so long ago it stopped talking. The ego has made it shy, but it is there, and it is powerful.

This voice says things like "That's not true. I am not stupid; I just made a mistake. I am human, and I am supposed to make mistakes. I can learn from what I just did. I can remember that and try not to do it again. I can make amends. I am good. I am doing the best I can. I am sorry; I was wrong, but I am not bad. I did a good job. What do you need right now? Tell me and I'll try to give it to you." This esteeming voice also says, "I love you. You have great worth. You deserve it. Thank you for being you. You are terrific, great, wonderful, clever, sweet, caring. That was a good thing you did. Don't you feel good? You are. You get a reward. What do you want?"

The esteeming voice is very powerful, for it is the voice of your true Self. It is far more powerful than the ego's voice because it is connected to your true feelings and your soul. This is why the ego does not want you to hear it. (Remember, the ego does not want to lose its power over you.) This is a positive, encouraging, loving, empowering, and empathetic voice. It is a balanced voice; like the Buddha, it has equal parts rationality and compassion. It is an honest voice that will not deceive you. If deceit is involved, it is the ego's voice.

What is the lesson? A teaching story

All the teaching stories used in this book are Oriental stories that have been told for centuries to illustrate a concept, or capture a significant truth, or symbolize a particular lesson. Thus, they are both simple and complex, clear and esoteric, difficult and easy—all at the same time. For they often present something paradoxical, something that is not the usual way of thinking, something that is upsetting or worrying. A good teaching story can be compared with a nut or a kernel: In order to get to the meat— the heart of the matter—one must work to break the shell or husk. Then the message has meaning; then it becomes personally relevant. This next story seems to encapsulate the very essence of the virtue of integrity, which requires moving past the ego, recognizing the true Self, and becoming aware of the soul's connection to the Whole. Remember, the ego contains all our desires for worldly recognition and comfort and therefore all our fears and insecurities; the soul only desires connection and reunification and therefore has no fear.

THERE ONCE WAS a Chinese Warlord who hated with a passion the religious orders in China. He made it his life's work to find and kill as many monks as he could. After slaughtering hundreds of monks in his province, the Warlord traveled to the outskirts of his territory. There he learned that a lone monk resided all by himself. Immediately upon hearing this, the Warlord went to the little temple and found the monk standing alone. In all his battle finery the Warlord strode up to the monk, pulled out his sword, and looked menacingly at the frail old man dressed in a simple robe. Surprisingly the monk seemed unafraid.

"Don't you know who I am?" the Warlord asked. "I can run this sword through your body without blinking an eye."

Looking the Warlord straight in the face, the old monk replied, "Don't you know who I am? I can let you run your sword through my body without blinking an eye."

The degree to which I trust myself
is the degree to which I am moral.

3
———

THE THIRD STEP:
Morality

SHE WAS ONE of the most moral human beings I have ever known. As a child I knew of her mostly from stories that I heard, but as an adult I began to know her for herself. I discovered that she was an incredible and unusual being. She was consistently and always exactly who she was: honest (sometimes unbearably so), dependable, loyal, brave, funny, sincere, and real. One always knew where one stood with her; one always knew exactly what her opinions were. Yet, and this is unusual, she always assumed full responsibility for her feelings and actions. She was the least attached human being I have ever known—to her desires, wants, or needs. In short, she was a woman of great integrity.

Her later years were remarkable for their simplicity and ordinariness. Content to bask in the limelight of others, she was self-effacing and unusually self-contained and disciplined. It took very little to make her happy. However, her life was not mundane, for she had "a past." As a young woman she had fallen in love with a married man who returned her love. This sounds like a fairly common story, except that her lover's wife was permanently confined to a mental hospital. Nowadays this would not be quite so tragic, given the sexual liberation and moral freedom that prevail. But back then, when she was young, this was tragedy. To compound the situation, all three participants were Catholic, meaning there could be no easy solution.

This affair continued for forty years, yet no one except the closest of family knew. The couple was discreet, the meetings were out of town on weekends, and the weekdays were spent in separate lives. There was great concern that no one be hurt, that no one be humiliated or embarrassed, that no harm be done. However, her situation was pure and simple adultery, and adultery is clearly immoral, as we all have learned. And yet, I repeat, she was one of the most moral beings I have known.

What is morality?

Morality is closely related to integrity, yet there are clear distinctions between the two virtues. Perhaps the simplest of these is that integrity can be thought of as who you are (beyond the ego) while morality involves what you do with who you are. In other words, integrity is your character; morality is the conduct of your character. The latter is most often associated with and defined by sexual conduct or following the rules of the community, but in reality morality is much larger: It concerns what is right and wrong in all areas of life.

The classic definitions deal with moral quality or character and being in accord with the standards, ethics, or principles involving right or wrong conduct. These definitions assume that being moral requires the capability to make the distinction between right and wrong actions and, even more specifically, to be virtuous in sexual conduct. Therefore, being a moral person implies conformity to generally accepted standards or principles of goodness or rightness in conduct or character. It is this conformity with society's ethics that usually determines whether or not someone is considered moral or immoral. It is also this conformity—the following of the predetermined rules set by the culture—that is believed necessary to prevent chaos and the disintegration of society.

Why is morality important?

Unlike all other animals who rely on instinct to determine their accepted means of behavior, man with his undeveloped instincts must rely on something else in order to live in society or become "civilized." This something else is custom or conformity with the accepted laws governing behavior. Man is both an individual and a social animal; he has needs to be both self-reliant and part of the group. These conflicting desires—to be separate and to be connected—are the foundation of the need for morality.

In his book *The Religions of Man,* Huston Smith states that the greatest impact in this area comes from the Hebraic codes of moral behavior, the Ten Commandments. Because these have been adopted by both the Christian and Islamic religions, they affect a significant number of the world's population. They form the basis for how to deal with the four problematic areas of living in a society; these four danger zones and how they are controlled are found in all human cultures. Man's appetites in the areas of force, wealth, sex, and the spoken word can quickly and easily lead to the dissolution of society unless they are diligently restrained. The Ten Commandments are explicit in addressing man's desires in these areas of conflict: "Thou shalt not murder," "Thou shalt not steal," "Thou shalt not commit adultery," and "Thou shalt not bear false witness" form the ethical cornerstones of all civilizations and religions.

In dealing with this topic, Huston Smith is most eloquent: "The importance of the Ten Commandments in their ethical dimension lies not in their uniqueness but in their universality, not in their finality but in their inescapable priority. They do not speak the final word in any area they touch; they speak instead the first word which must be spoken if other words are to follow."

How is morality developed?

Initially humans relied on spontaneous tradition, the social mores that were tried and proved and handed down from generation to generation in order to maintain the cohesiveness of their society. But as man became more progressive and self-reliant, these established behavioral patterns were no longer sufficient to hold the group together. When self-consciousness replaced group consciousness, when reason replaced habit, and when self-interest replaced the group norms, other means besides spontaneous tradition had to be employed in order to maintain the integrity of the collective group. Examples of other means include the use of reason, the use of stringent control and severe punishments, and the use of the power of love to control.

We may indeed relate to the need for a stronger morality in America today, but this is not the first time that there has been a breakdown in the social cohesion of a culture. A good example of a society's dissolution and loss of cohesion existed in China from the twelfth to the third century before Christ. During the fourth century B.C. China was in such a state of turbulence and constant warfare that the stage was set for dramatic social and moral change. Onto this stage came Confucius, not a religious leader or a politician, but rather a humble and simple teacher who revolutionized not only China itself but our modern concepts of morality. Confucius developed a philosophy designed to cohere China; he created a deliberate and powerful tradition that continues to this day.

He began by deciding what values were critical for the well-being of the society, and then he implemented these values through every possible means of education until they became internalized by everyone in the society. Confucius actually brainwashed an entire culture through the use of written history, stories and proverbs, schools, toys, homes, theaters, and temples. In short, all formal and informal means of teaching were employed. A carefully calculated and planned tradition was invented, and the dissemination of this tradition was just as carefully controlled. What Confucius did was indeed remarkable because instead of relying on spontaneous and therefore haphazard customs of accepted behavior, he created a "deliberate tradition" and kept it strong through education and attention to its fulfillment of specific goals for character development and the conduct of social life.

Two basic principles are important to understanding how Confucius viewed the concept of morality. First, he believed that there could be no social or political harmony unless there was first moral harmony within the self. His creation of this moral harmony was relatively simple; he used anecdotes and moral sayings to reinforce his core values. Two examples of these, related to the concept of virtue, are: "Feel kindly with everyone, but be intimate only with the virtuous," and "A man without virtue cannot long abide adversity, nor can he long abide in happiness."

Second, Confucius defined morality through conformity to the set values or standards. This conformity was achieved through careful delineation of five areas of human relationships and the proper conduct of behavior for each. The comportment of each person in the midst of his relationships determines his destiny, and the secret of proper conduct is found in the concept of empathy. Thus, "A sound man's heart is not shut into itself but is open to the hearts of others; it will feel their heartbeats as if it were his own," and "Answer hatred with justice and love with benevolence. Otherwise, you would waste your benevolence."

Why is morality more than conformity?

Confucianism is clearly concerned with the state of the individual self, but only so far as this leads to cultural conformity. It views the means to become a moral person as the foundation for the proper way to behave in relationships and in society. This is its primary goal of morality—not as a virtue for the individual but as a requirement for the culture. Therefore, to our modern Western eyes, it may seem too confining, and too structured for our individualistic tastes. We tend to resent being told what to do and how to do it, particularly in terms of our personal relationships.

The idea of having a deliberate tradition forced upon us is not tenable for a culture based on individual liberty. We simply value our independence and free will too strongly. Besides, we have painfully learned that blind obedience to cultural norms often absolves individuals from taking personal responsibility for their actions. In fact, very strong moral dictates frequently lead to the very things they are trying to prevent: perversions and immoral behavior. When the society's codes of conduct are too rigidly imposed, the individual becomes repressed and often acts out in secrecy. A good example of this existed in Victorian England with its unusually large amount of child abuse and sexual perversions.

And herein lies the difficulty because the concept of morality, which is a human virtue, has become synonymous with conformity, which is a societal necessity. The foundation for all definitions and descriptions of morality is contained in the myths, stories, history, and traditions that construct our connections to the past and to one another. We learn what is moral from our cultures, religions, laws, and rules; we learn that what is immoral is what is different. As the German philosopher Schopenhauer said, "Every man takes the limits of his own field of vision for the limits of the world."

Because our egos need limits in order to feel secure, we construct moral boundaries based on conformity with what we have been culturally taught: What we believe is right, good, just, and moral; anything that opposes our beliefs must then be wrong, bad, unjust, and immoral. Thus, we become judges and governors of others' morality; we become prejudiced, closed, and rejecting. Judging others by their sexual choices or proclivities seems to be a national pastime; gossiping and denigrating those who are different or nonconforming is considered a natural component of the work or group culture. These activities may indeed feel "normal" because they are so familiar, but are they moral? Do they bring out the best in us? Or do they instead feed the ego's need to belong, to be similar, to be accepted?

Conformity taken to extremes becomes biased and judgmental; in the rigidly moral system, conformity often culminates in immorality. This occurs whenever a group feels justified, based solely on its power, to take the law into its own hands and create violence, destruction, and even death. Look at what occurred in Germany under the Nazi regime; what happened in South Africa under apartheid; what is happening right now in Northern Ireland, Bosnia, the Middle East, Iraq, Iran, and Russia and here in the United States whenever racial tensions are provoked.

In order to avoid the problem of conformity leading to evil, we must stop being dependent upon any system or group to determine our personal values. This means that we no longer rely on habits or customs to determine our behaviors. But in giving up our conformity, we cannot give up our morality. Therefore, the answer to this dilemma means that we need to separate the two and rediscover morality as separate from conformity.

Why is morality a virtue?

While morality certainly is manifested through our behavior toward others and our connection with our society, it is not limited only to these external actions and interactions. Rather, morality is best understood as the outward reflection of our inner beings; it is the mirror of our own integrity. Therefore, it is a much more complicated and involved process than simply conforming to the accepted standards of behavior within the society. It cannot exist separately from the self; it is only superficial if determined simply by following the rules or going along with the tribe.

Morality as a personal virtue is strongly related to the

cardinal virtue of temperance, meaning moderation, restraint, control, renunciation, denial, and especially *self-control* and *self-discipline.* To a lesser degree, it is related to the concept of chastity or being pure, decent, modest, and clean. Purity and cleanliness in this case do not refer to the external body but to the internal being. Thus, the virtue of morality that is needed is the ability to be "clean" with the self, to find the purity that exists beyond the ego, the ability to control the appetites and desires of the ego, and, above all, to do it for the Self. In other words, morality means doing the best you can as much as you can because you want to do so for yourself. It requires replacing what you "should" do according to others with what you want to do according to your true Self.

What is my first moral duty?

Your first duty is not to others or to society or even to God. Your first duty is to yourself. This may sound exactly the opposite from what is taught, but it lies at the foundation of all the major world religions. From the Hindus, Swami Vivekananda writes: "Our first duty is not to hate ourselves; to advance [to God] we must have faith in ourselves first and then in God. He who has no faith in himself can never have faith in God. The gate to degeneration opens when a man begins to hate himself." From Islam, an Arab mystic says, "To mount to God is to enter into oneself." The Buddha preached: "Do not accept tradition—be ye lamps unto yourself. Have Self as a lamp,

Self as a refuge, and no other refuge." From Christianity, St. Augustine proclaims, "The good which I now sought was not outside myself. . . . For those who try to find joy in things outside themselves easily vanish away into emptiness."

Once you realize that the essence of virtue lies in the way you feel about yourself, you become the supreme authority over your own behavior. When you can love yourself, everything that you do will come from that love. So if your first duty is to love your Self, your second duty must be to act out of that loved and loving Self. Then your morality, along with all your other virtues, is simply part of your being, part of who you are and what you do. You no longer need rules, traditions, laws, and customs in order to be "good" because you have a higher and truer authority, the goodness that is the foundation of your inner being. The authority of the world is based on the world's insecurity and needs for power and control; this is the domain of the weak ego or the collective weak egos known as society. The authority that you recognize, once you have learned to love, respect, and trust your Self, is based on the only true security that exists, the security of the inner Self.

Why is morality so difficult?

As soon as we discover this inner authority, we also discover that the concepts of duty and morality are not fixed but instead vary under differing circumstances. What once seemed so simple now can be very complex. Our lives are constantly being tested by situations and events that do not conform to simple definitions of duty and morality. We know it is wrong to kill, but what about doing so in order to survive? We know it's wrong to steal, but what are business takeovers doing? And suppose we need that job that has been "stolen" from a former employee? We know it's wrong to lie, but what do we do when being honest would cause great and unnecessary pain? And what about the adulterers mentioned in the beginning of this chapter? Was their forty-year love immoral?

There are many historical examples of those who go against the moral standards of their cultures but are considered heroes. Take Robin Hood and the Nazi resistance movement as a start. How about Vietnam? Who was moral? Those who went and fought or those who resisted and ran away? There are also more recent examples of extremely complicated moral issues: The Gulf War; the antiabortionists who believe so strongly in the rights of the unborn child that they kill those in opposition; the death penalty—all these and more are ever-present and complicated moral situations. Who determines the morality in each situation? Who is the judge, the final authority?

How do we know what is right and what is wrong for ourselves when in one case a behavior is called moral while in another case the same behavior is called immoral? The answer to this dilemma is found only when you trust your true Self. Then you will immediately know when you have done something wrong because you will feel bad about yourself. Likewise, you will know when you are right because you will feel good about yourself. This is different from the process that occurs when the ego is in charge. Then you will look to others in order to know if what you have done is right or wrong. You will rank the opinion of others over your own conscience. A good example of trusting yourself occurs when you learn to value truth over honesty. Being true to yourself, who you are and what you are, is far more important than adhering to a policy of complete honesty. Using honesty as an excuse to hurt someone is not moral. Furthermore, honesty can often be situational and dependent upon your emotional state ("I hate you when I'm mad at you"); your feelings will pass, but your true Self remains constant ("I love you, but my ego hates you when you don't obey me. This is my problem, not yours").

These distinctions become even more difficult when we realize that the ego is always playing games with our minds and twisting things around in order to satisfy its desires and needs. The ego is weak and without substance or real power; it is based on illusion—the illusion that it is the self—and it gains its power and control from sustaining that illusion, convincing both ourselves and others that it is important and real, and seeking validation and acceptance from external sources. The weak ego encourages us to do exactly what we want to do in order to get its needs met, and then it turns on us and tells us that we are evil, immoral, and worthless.

What is the immoral path?
The weak ego does not believe that we are good or that our goodness comes from God and does not have to be worked for or earned. As soon as we realize this, we can begin to have a relationship with the soul; we are ready to recognize that inside each of us exists a very pure and holy part of our being. The ego is in competition with the soul and knows that we will pay attention to either the one or the other. Thus, it demands all our attention and enlists our monkey minds to help it get our concentration. When it succeeds and we attend only to it, it gains strength over us and we lose control over the Self and our connection to the soul. Then the ego goes out of control. This is manifested by unlimited and incessant desires and needs, which must be fulfilled at all costs. No matter what we do, how much we get, or how often we get it, the weak ego demands more, more, more. There is never going to be enough.

Now is precisely the time when we become vulnerable to becoming immoral. In this process (the ego's development of power), we believe that only the ego's demands are relevant, and so we lose our connection to the conscience, our own personal moral guide. We simply stop listening to any restraining or oppositional (to the ego) voices within us. Next, we begin to lose our virtue, the awareness of our goodness, because all our effort and energy are spent trying to satisfy these ever-increasing ego demands. In effect, we are severing our connection to the soul. In short, the uncontrolled ego is evil; the self controlled entirely by this ego is immoral. This immorality may be demonstrated in our behaviors and relationships with others—our society—but it is first apparent in our feelings toward our true Selves. We have shirked our first duty; we hate ourselves.

When is morality not moral?

By understanding the process of the ego's development of power and control over the Self, we begin to comprehend the immense complexity involved in being a moral person. When we reflect on our lives, we can see that we have never completely followed the rules and that we have used denial, anxiety, fear, rationalization, projection, and all the other defense mechanisms in order to sustain our facades and appear to be good and acceptable to others. We may have fooled some of them, but we surely have not fooled ourselves. We know we have conflicting wants: We want to be good, and we want to have our desires satisfied. It is in trying to have both wants met that we get into murky waters. And it is exactly this murkiness that prevents us from journeying inside; we simply are afraid of what we will find in our inner beings. How much easier it is to avoid this painful journey and focus on something else. Of course the easiest path of avoidance is projection, putting our insecurities onto others.

We recognize that our own morality is complex, but we still find the morality of others to be simple to determine. It is so much easier to judge others than it is to be "clean" with ourselves. It seems so natural and normal to think about and discuss what someone else should or should not be doing; it is much more difficult to focus continually on what we are doing. It is seductive to try to have others conform to our standards; it is hard work to keep ourselves conforming to the high standards of the true Self. And even when we manage to focus on the Self and constrain the ego, we will still encounter difficulties. For it is not our task to judge others, no matter how truthful and moral we are being with ourselves. It is our task to accept others, even when they are not conforming to what we believe is right for us. We must accept others in the condition in which they exist, rather than in the state we would choose for them. The most we can do is judge their behavior but never their being. And this is very difficult.

What is my responsibility?

The Western world does not have a counterpart for the Eastern concept of karma; the most we have is a fuzzy concept of fate or luck. We tend to think of karma as predestination implying determinism and a lack of control over our lives and to reject the notion because it opposes our concept of free will. The word *karma* actually means "work," and the doctrine refers to a moral law of cause and effect. What this doctrine entails is complete personal responsibility for all actions. Everything we do, all our actions (our work) create future consequences. Thus, karma means action, and all action has reaction. It is as if what we do today creates seeds that will sprout tomorrow. In this doctrine each individual is responsible for his present condition (based on what has been done in the past) and is creating the future that he deserves. Whether or not this is a usable doctrine for us, its essence is important: We are responsible for our actions. Thus we control our behavior and are accountable for the consequences.

The relationship between judging others and the concept of karma is clear. We are responsible for what we do; others are responsible for what they do. We are not responsible for what others do (provided they are not dependent upon us), and they are not responsible for us. Therefore, there is no point in blaming others for what we are feeling, thinking, doing, or being, and there is also no point in becoming preoccupied with what they are doing. It is a waste of time to worry about or criticize what others are doing; this is time to be spent working on the Self and one's own behavior. Just as our first duty is to ourselves, the first duty of others is to themselves. If they do not want to recognize this, we have a moral obligation to allow them to be without our interference unless they have asked us for help. Each of us is on our own path; we cannot be on more than one path at a time. Therefore, we need to stay on our own paths in life and stay off others' paths. Again from Buddha: "Every individual must tread the path to the end of suffering himself through his own energy and initiative—work out your own salvation with diligence."

How do I practice being moral?

Perhaps the simplest way to internalize the virtue of morality is to be as true to your complete Self as you possibly can be as often as you possibly can. Being true to the Self, or being clean with yourself, implies a clear connection to all aspects of yourself with the conscious exclusion of the ego (as much as possible). This may actually be easier to do than it is to describe. The simplest way to practice being connected to yourself and having your doing and your being integrated is continually to ask yourself this question: "How do I feel about myself right now?" Anytime you are involved in doing something, any moment that you can take a pause, anyplace that you are by yourself or with others, take a few seconds to ask this question of yourself. Then wait for the answer. The ego will try to distract you by questioning the question: "Why are you asking that?"; "Don't you know how you feel?"; "What a stupid thing to do"; and so on. Ignore the ego; tell it to "shut up"; laugh at it, and ask the question anyway. This simple little question will put you in touch with your true Self more quickly than any self-development workshop, book, or even meditation. Ask the question, and wait for the answer from within.

In the beginning you may find that it takes a while for an answer to come, or you may even get an "I don't know." Respect the process, and understand that as with any new relationship, it takes time to establish easy and spontaneous communication. You are communicating with your true Self—your connection to your soul—and if this is new, your Self may not be used to being heard. Keep asking and keep waiting. You will hear the answer, and sometimes you will be surprised at what you hear. If your ego has controlled you for a long time, the answer you get may be the opposite of what you expect. Trust the answer; it is the real you talking.

With practice, you will move beyond the "I don't know" answer, and you will discover that there are only two possible answers. One is "I feel good about me," and the other is "I feel bad about me." Everything important that you think, believe, and do can be assessed by this criterion: "How does this make me feel about my Self?" The weak ego hates this simple little question; it much prefers "How do they feel about me?" or "How do I feel about them?" These questions do absolutely nothing for the Self or the encouragement of virtue, except perhaps indicate that changes need to be made and work needs to be done.

Once you have heard the answer, you will know what to do. If the answer is "I feel good," continue what you are doing. This is simple. If the answer is "I feel bad," stop doing (or thinking) whatever, and change your behavior. Stop as soon as you know you are doing something that is going against your Self. It is better to do nothing rather than to keep moving away from your goodness. Remember karma, and think of your behavior as little seeds; you will not want to create future consequences from behaviors that work against you. If you are not sure what to do once you have ceased your negative behavior (negative to your true Self), ask yourself what would make you feel good about yourself, and try to do that.

Repeat this exercise all the time. It does not take much time, and with practice it takes even less time. But it has tremendous long-term benefits because it keeps you straight with yourself; it allows you to trust yourself. It keeps you connected to your conscience and your soul; it keeps you ringing true. You are the authority of your Self; you are responsible for your Self. You create an integrated and whole being, not from some tremendous or cataclysmic event, but from monitoring the small steps of your everyday life. With practice, you will realize Shakespeare's meaning when he said: "To thine own self be true."

What is the lesson? A teaching story
The moral of the following story may be the easiest of all the stories to grasp, but simple as it may be to understand, this is one of the most difficult concepts to practice.

Therein lies the rub because the virtue of morality is found in the practice—in the observed behaviors and the spoken thoughts and shared ideas. Morality is how you live your goodness, how your true Self behaves in the world. Thus, it is the acid test of how your integrity handles your often conflicting needs to belong.

ONE DAY TWO monks from a celibate order were taking a trip across their country and came to a flooded river. There they saw a lone woman struggling fruitlessly to get across the river. It was obvious that she could not do so without help. One of the monks approached her and asked if she needed assistance.

"Yes, please," she replied, "for I cannot get across by myself."

The monk then proceeded to pick her up and carry her across the river, where he set her down on the opposite side. She thanked him profusely and went on her way. The two monks also continued on their journey. After a few hours of travel it became obvious to the helpful monk that his companion was furious. Finally, when the companion could no longer fume in silence, he exploded at the other.

"Why did you do that? You know we have pledged to have nothing to do with women. How could you pick her up and carry her across the river? Are you crazy? What has happened to your vows?"

To which the accused monk quietly replied: "I put my woman down hours ago. When are you going to let go of yours?"

The degree to which I live my goodness
is the degree to which I am creative.

4

THE FOURTH STEP:
Creativity

ONCE I HAD a client who was quite a well-known painter. He came to therapy in noisy desperation and told of years of abuse and self-destruction. He had tried drugs and been rehabilitated; he had abused alcohol and was in recovery. He had been treated for depression, for manic episodes, for childhood abuse, and for relationship problems. He spoke of having an identity disorder, of not being sure of either his sexuality or his sexual identity. He considered himself a mess, but he knew that he was a good artist.

As we progressed together in the therapy, we discovered that he believed that all his problems, all his dysfunctional behaviors, and all his addictions were part of his self-perception of being a creative person. He was afraid to become balanced and integrated; he felt that being at peace with himself would stop his creative energy and that he would lose the one thing he did well. After all, he told me, almost every artist or creative person whom he knew was self-destructive. "Don't the two go together?" he asked.

His question was a good one, for there is a long history of association between artists and mental problems. For the past several hundred years, since the Romantic movement, creativity has been linked with pain, unhappiness, insecurity, and problems in dealing with life in a constructive manner. There exists an unfortunate assumption that the creation of something beautiful requires the destruction of the self; sensitivity requires and is demonstrated through suffering. In other words, we must give up part of our being—the balanced, peaceful, and connected part—in order to have the energy to be creative. Thus, uncovering my client's fear of losing his artistry if he became healthy made sense.

Fortunately he was a risk taker and was willing to try another path in his pilgrimage. It also helped when I pointed out that he could always revert to his previous patterns, that regression is much easier than progression. But the real clincher and the turning point in his therapy occurred when he discovered that the most creative thing that anyone can do in life is to become balanced and integrated. It simply requires great creativity to be in this world and to be connected to what is not immediately evident or visible. The only way to do so is to love your Self and to realize and demonstrate your goodness (your connection to God), and doing this, because of all the training to the contrary, may be at the heart of creativity. Incidentally, he succeeded in his quest and discovered that he was an even better artist than he had believed himself to be. His paintings changed as they reflected his inner peace and balance and became truly wonderful, full of wonder.

What is creativity?

We know that the word *creative* means "bringing into being" and that the concept of being creative implies being original, unique, and inventive. Thus, creativity entails the willingness or ability to try something new, to shift paradigms and expand conventional boundaries. We may not be as familiar with the idea that creativity involves dedicating oneself to something larger than oneself and moving beyond the limitations of the familiar—the rational, the logical, the conventional, and, most personally, the ego-self.

The creative approach is usually the opposite of the more rational or scientific approach because it is involved with the illumination of principles and not the accumulation of facts. The rigor and repetition of scientific method are the kiss of death to creativity, which requires spontaneous and unrestrained energy. When this energy becomes standardized, by definition originality is stifled. Peak experiences and flow cannot occur in a count, weigh, and measure environment.

At its essence creativity is the union of opposites, the balance between the rational and the compassionate, the objective and the subjective, the known and the unknown. Its spontaneous energy is derived from the tension or uncertainty of recognizing that there are no polarities, that life means death, that sickness and health are related, that good and bad, right and wrong are part of the same pattern. The rational mind can conceive of this pattern and see that everything is related; the compassionate heart can feel the pain that is inherent. The balance between the two is the basis for all creativity.

Therefore, creativity is not purely subjective but does have some objective reality. If it were only subjective, it would exist in the domain of the ego and quickly become self-serving (ego-fulfilling). True creativity transcends the ego; it contributes something new and changes the culture. In his book *Creativity* Mihaly Csikszentmihalyi differentiates it from talent, which is the ability to do something well, and from the personal ability to experience the world in novel ways. This is the difference between something that is good and something that is truly great: the hundreds of Greek and Roman sculptures in museums throughout the world versus Michelangelo's David; the thousands of good war and romance novels versus *Gone with the Wind;* most music versus Mozart or the Beatles.

How is creativity created?

Almost all of us have had moments that we know are different, that seem to have removed us from place and time. Such moments have been called flow or peak experiences or natural highs. These moments are often associated with the creative process, and while they can occur without this association, creativity does not occur without them. The most important quality of the creative process, the one that is consistently present, is the ability to enjoy the process of creation, not for what it will lead to but for what is occurring in the moment. In other words, being creative means being in flow.

In trying to describe the creative process for his book, Csikszentmihalyi listed five steps that traditionally occur. They consist of preparation, incubation (letting ideas churn subconsciously), insight (the "ha" moment), evaluation, and elaboration (time and hard work). These steps are not a linear process, but rather involve consistent repetition. Problems and suffering seem to be inherent to the process, but they actually are necessary and help the creative outcome. What is important to recognize here is that creative processes involve far more than the moment of insight; like genius, as Edison stated, they are 1 percent inspiration and 99 percent perspiration.

Perhaps even more relevant for understanding this virtue are Csikszentmihalyi's findings on what constitutes the creative person. He describes such people as able to find purpose and enjoyment in the chaos of existence. They are remarkable in their ability to adapt to any situation and to use whatever is available to achieve their goals. As expected, they are curious about, interested in, and full of wonder toward the world around them, how things work and what things are. In attempting to describe such personalities with one word, Csikszentmihalyi chose *com-*

plexity. He defines a *complex personality* as one that is able to express all the traits and all the feelings that are available to humans. Creative individuals are good and bad, aggressive and cooperative, objective and subjective; they are fully rounded and not polarized by the usual dichotomous extremes. They are aware of their dark sides and are not afraid to be real and whole.

He goes on to list some of these extremes: great energy combined with periods of quiet, being both smart and naive, disciplined and playful, extroverted and introverted, realistic and imaginative, and humble and proud; being androgynous (masculine and feminine), rebellious and traditional, objective and passionate, and able both to suffer and to enjoy. As he states, "Creative persons definitely know both extremes and experience both with equal intensity and without inner conflict." This is a critical revelation, for what it means is that the truly creative individual accepts his inconsistencies; he moves beyond a stereotyped role. In other words, he is able to move beyond the imposed limitations of the weak ego and to experience the true Self, in all its complexity. Two examples of such complexity are Mother Teresa and Katharine Hepburn. While very different in style and purpose, they are similar in that both are known for being real. Neither can be stereotyped to a particular situation or circumstance; they demonstrate the transcendence of roles and the realization of the true Selves.

What is the relationship
between creativity and religion?

There is more than a casual relationship between these two topics. Up until the past few centuries, the mechanistic and scientific eras, all creative endeavors were dedications to God. Art was created to glorify and explain the Divine. Paintings and sculptures had the purpose not to decorate but to illuminate religious themes; the absence of printed matter meant that pictures told the stories. Music, dance, drama, prose, and poetry were associated with religious themes and the goal of teaching goodness. This can readily be seen in India, Egypt, the Far East, Africa, and the cathedrals of Europe, as well as in all primitive and ethnic cultures. Even today there are some cultures in which no distinction is made between creativity and religion; for example, the Balinese religion requires some form of creative endeavor in all work. Perhaps the simplest explanation for this connection is found in the definition of creativity as the dedication to something greater than the self: the Creator.

Life has been described as a joint venture between the human and the Divine, the known and the mystical, reality and mystery. The concept of free will gives us the freedom to make choices; the ideal life means that we can choose what both works for us as humans and honors that which is sacred. This is no easy task and requires great creativity. All religions address this dilemma in some fashion.

Taoists believe that genuine creation combines supreme activity and supreme relaxation and that the only way to do this is to release the subconscious. The conscious mind (controlled by the ego) must relax, let go, and stop standing in its own light. An important Tao concept is wu wei, or creative quietude. This can occur only when the private ego and the conscious mind yield to a greater power not their own. This creative quietude also reflects the union of opposites, the interconnection of the yin and the yang.

In the Islam faith the Sufis try to make Allah a reality in their everyday life; their twirling dance is a type of meditation designed to bring them to a state of mysticism, an altered state of consciousness, an entering into a greater form of reality. The rituals found in all religions are related to the creative experience known as flow; their purpose is to rise above the ordinary, the everyday routine, and into a higher form of communication or relationship. One of the most creative constructs of this ideal is exemplified by the Zen Buddhists, who try to bring enlightenment (the other world) into this world in every moment of daily life. The purpose of Zen practice is to have no conflict, no obstruction between the two worlds—the human and the Divine. Their goal is to find the mystical in the ordinary, to bring the glow of experience into everyday activities.

Perhaps one of the best examples of creativity in religion can be found in Judaism. The God of the Jews, unlike the amoral and indifferent gods of their

Mediterranean contemporaries, was perceived, according to theologian Huston Smith, "as a God of unutterable greatness and holiness," meaning that He was both highly moral and extremely loving. "In the beginning God created the heavens and the earth," begins the Old Testament, and with it the concept that life has meaning and that humans have worth. When faith is lost, according to Judaism, the fault is not life itself or God because it is man himself who gives the meaning to his life. This simple concept gives us the freedom to be creative and change, rather than to be passive and blame.

From the very beginning, so the Jewish tribe believes, Yahweh has been taking care of them and commanding them to follow His lead. This has led to a unique intimacy with God that is not as readily apparent in other traditions. This relationship has been demonstrated by communications between God and the prophets, from Abraham to Moses to Amos, Hosea, Isaiah, Jeremiah, and others. In these communications, God has spoken— sometimes in anger and sometimes in stillness, sometimes with symbols (the burning bush) and sometimes with words (the Ten Commandments). As a result of this history of interactions with the Divine, Jews expected to suffer; this was part of God's plan. They learned to view suffering not merely as a punishing but as a teaching experience for them and a redemptive one for the world. It is interesting to note that this perception of pain and suffering is very similar to the description of the creative individual as one who perceives problems and miseries as inherent, challenging, and necessary aspects of the creative process.

Why is creativity a virtue?

All religions agree that it is much more difficult to live in the world and worship God; it seems much easier to give up trying to fathom that which cannot be known and to live without God. It is also much easier to be tragic than to be hopeful. Discouragement and negativity simply require less effort and energy than do encouragement and faith. Feeling fulfilled and peaceful in the midst of pain and difficulty requires creativity, courage, and strength. It is exactly this that connects creativity to the cardinal virtue of fortitude. The creative process is not a speedy one, the creative path is not easy, but creativity is the only way to enhance one's experience. To discover the meaning in the experience requires vigor, vitality (love of life), and endurance. As the British writer Aldous Huxley stated, "Experience is not what happens to you; it is what you do with what happens to you."

Nothing stops creativity as surely as fear. The ego uses fear to keep it secure and dominant. The fears of rejection, alienation, ridicule, and separation are basic human ones that must be overcome for a person to be creative. The very basis for creativity is the detachment from the norm, the commonplace, the accepted. The weak ego is terrified of such detachment because it yearns for attachment and approval at all times. It is very difficult to be the best that one can be and ignore the sneers and discouragement of others. It is much simpler to be reactive rather than creative. Being aware of others' reactions stops the creative process. Being in flow requires having a dialogue with the true Self, the connection to the soul; there will always be those who will not let flow occur, either for themselves or for others.

One of the surest ways to stop creativity is with sophistication, cynicism, and rationality. These unfortunately are much more common responses than their opposites: naïveté and wonder, support and imagination. The world will not make it easy to be creative; furthermore, strict adherence to organized religion will actually prevent the creative process from occurring. As the modern scholar Joseph Campbell explained, "In all traditional systems . . . the authorized mythological forms are presented in rites to which the individual is expected to respond with an experience of commitment and belief." But what happens if he doesn't have such an experience, if he doesn't believe? How, then, is he supposed to behave? Campbell continues: "The normal way is to fake it, to feel oneself to be inadequate, to pretend to believe, to strive to believe, and to live in the imitation of others, an inauthentic life. The authentic creative way, on the other hand, which I would term the way of art as opposed to religion, is, rather, to reverse this authoritative order." In other words, instead of starting to believe from the outside—the externals, the rites—we must begin inside with the internals—our spirits and souls. But to make matters even more difficult, our own egos will try to prevent this; they will restrict our creativity because of fear of rejection from the external world. Therefore, being creative becomes a virtue, a challenge, something to strive for and encourage within ourselves.

Because the driving force behind creativity is the love of the thing rather than the results, being creative requires becoming detached from the ego, which is always concerned with goals and outcomes. The secret behind creativity lies in realizing that it is not what is done but how it is done that is critical. The ego's driving concern is always what is done; therefore, creativity requires moving past our restrictive egos. This move past the ego has been described by the novelist Richard Stern as "getting lost" in the creative process: "At your best you're not thinking. . . . You're not an ego at that point. It's not competitive. . . . I would use the word pure. You know that this is right. I don't mean that it works in the world, or that it adds up, but that it's right in this place. . . ." The process he describes is the true essence of creativity, the loss of ego and discovery of the Divine.

Why am I a creative being?
You know that the simplest description of creativity means the causing or coming into existence or the bringing into *being*. It also means making, producing, or inventing. You

probably associate creativity with something artistic or original or unique, but the virtue of creativity lies in the fact that you are continually creating your Self. Just the fact that you are alive and changing means that you are always adapting, acting, and inventing yourself. The paintings of my client are not nearly as creative as he himself is; this book is not as creative as I my Self is. You also are always involved in the process of creating and re-creating yourself every minute of your life, and as soon as you recognize your connection to the Creator, you will recognize as well the fact that you are a co-creator. You are making your life what it is; you are choosing to realize your potential, to become who you really are. You are the maker of your destiny, the producer of your life, the inventor of yourself. What can possibly be more creative than this?

Living is not easy; you easily recognize this overstated fact. You have been taught that power is control; you probably have learned that you cannot control very much. You may believe that your happiness and success are connected to others and things external to yourself, and now you must learn that this is not true. You search for safety and meaning and have been trained to look in all the wrong places before you discover that everything you seek is inside you. But no one tells you this when you are young and easily trainable. You discover this only when you are older and disillusioned and your brain has hardened. You may have spent decades working very hard in order to be approved by others, only to discover that your real worth is internal. You ache and you cry, you seek and become frustrated, and now you learn that what you have been looking for, what you really need, has always been inside you. You may think that it is all a cosmic joke and that the joke is on you. And yet you have persevered, you have survived. How can you doubt your creative abilities?

Everything you are, everything you have done smack of being creative. Nothing that is externally produced is as interesting as what you are now producing. This has long been recognized by indigenous cultures in their storytelling. Your life is a story, and you are constantly creating these marvelous stories, most often without recognition or realization. It is simply much easier to turn the responsibility for your life over to someone else or even to God. Discovering that you have equal responsibility for your life—that you are indeed a *co-creator*—may initially seem overwhelming. Yet this is what every creator of anything knows: You put your name on what you do; you take credit for what you have created. Thus, you change your focus. It is not that life is happening to you; it is rather that you are happening to it.

Why is creativity so difficult?

You know that you are alive and that you are also dying; because you are mortal, you recognize that everything you are experiencing is temporary. You also know that nothing drives you as strongly or as clearly as your fears. You want to know; you want to be safe; you yearn for stability and permanence. You develop your ego to separate and individuate yourself from others; this is a necessary developmental process. Then one day you discover that this same ego hampers and inhibits you. You are told that love is the answer, but you have not been taught how to love without conditions. Instead you have learned to compete, to hate, to judge, to hide your imperfections and weaknesses in order to get ahead, to be a success. The life that you visibly see is not the life that will make you happy, you learn, but how do you trust what you cannot see?

All religions teach that God created you and then gave you free will, gave you the choice to do what you want. All religions speak of a God who loves you unconditionally, but then they compare this God with earthly fathers who are unable to love you unconditionally. And so you have learned that God must love us like our earthly fathers do, but this is not unconditional love. There is nothing human, nothing that you can rationally see or reasonably feel that conveys the concept of unconditional love—love without any requirements, boundaries, or needs. And so you must become very creative to try to understand a concept that is not easily understood, that stretches your imagination and exceeds your highest hopes and greatest fears.

How do I become a co-creator?

One source that answers this most relevant question is the powerful book *Conversations with God* by Neale Donald Walsch. It states that you begin co-creating as soon as you recognize that you are the creator of your reality. The first step in this process is your thought; it is the origin of all that follows. Thus, you begin creating when you think something into being because thought is pure energy. Every thought you have ever had and ever will have is creative; the energy of your thought will never cease to exist. Therefore, it is very important to understand the power of your thoughts. Next comes the word; everything that you say is an expressed thought. Finally comes action, which can be conceived of as the movement of your thoughts and words.

The beginning of everything, then, is the thought, and the end of it all is the action, just as the beginning is the Creator and the end is the Creator created or experienced. Therefore, everything you think, everything you say, and everything you do are involved in co-creating the reality of you. The purpose of it all is to create your experience, to create your Self, right here and right now. You are not living merely to learn because your soul knows it all; you are living to experience it all because then your soul will know it experientially. This is a much fuller, deeper, and richer knowledge that cannot be obtained by any other means. Therefore, what is happening to you, what you are experiencing, is your meaning, your reason, and your purpose.

The co-creation process is much simpler if you believe in the ultimate Creator, but even this is not strictly necessary. (It is not important that you believe in God; what is important is that God believes in you.) If faith is difficult for you, begin with the thought that you are good. Your goodness is given; it does not have to be achieved. When you start with this thought, you are starting with positive energy, and the words and actions that follow will also be positive. If, however, you begin with negativity—"I am bad; I have no worth"—your words and actions will increase the negative energy that you are putting out into the world. So begin with the positive.

Continue your creation of positive energy by speaking encouragingly, first to yourself and then with others. Speak the positive, the supportive; refrain from speaking the negative, the discouraging. Say aloud, "I am good. I have great worth. I deserve to be fulfilled, content, and at peace." Remember, it is never too late to change the energy, to reverse a negative process into a positive one, to create yourself as you truly are. Learn to bite your tongue in order to hold back the negativity, the judgmental, the easy biting comments that you have learned to make. Practice the positive, and soon it will seem natural and easy.

Finally, allow your behavior—your actions—to follow your thoughts and words. Again, this is much easier to do if you begin with yourself. When you know that you are good, it is natural to do those things that demonstrate this goodness. If you believe you are not good, your actions will reflect this destructive self-belief. You do not have to be stuck in a negative pattern; because you are choosing—creating—you have the final say in being who you truly are. You alone can choose what you do and how you do it. The world cannot create you; it can only respond to your creation of yourself. You cannot control this response, this reaction; you can control the action that puts everything in motion. It is your reality, your experience, your life. Choose wisely; choose what will best work for you. Choose how best to be your true Self.

*What is the difference
between creating and co-creating?*
I have been writing this book all my life. Bits and pieces of wisdom have been sticking to me just like cat hairs as long as I can remember. Stories I have heard, especially the teaching stories that Buzz used in his therapy, aphorisms, quotations, parts of novels, great literature, and even comic strips have stayed with me and sometimes haunted me with their meaning. Often the obvious has seemed mysterious when pondered, but sometimes, on blessed occasions, the mysterious has become obvious.

Long before I knew that I would write and years before I became published, I was writing this book in my mind, with my body and from my soul. I would find myself composing it as I lay in that magical place between sleep and consciousness. Sometimes I would wake up with perfectly formed sentences but without a context. I would find myself talking it, thinking it, and sometimes even spurting out something that had nothing to do with the ongoing conversation. I often and easily embarrassed my children with these outbursts; my patient husband is now used to them, and my soul friends encourage my digressions. But this book is bigger than I am and demands to be written; it bubbles up from within and has always been doing so.

Sitting in my brother's house in Italy writing the final chapter of my last book, I expected to feel the marvelous sense of relief that comes with completion. Instead I discovered that I was already working on this book. Now I am sitting in my house in Houston, and I am obsessed with it. As any writer will tell you, I often have grave doubts anyone else will want to read it. And then I remember: I want to read this book. I want to know how all the bits and pieces that I have been collecting and hoarding all my life will fit into this context. For I have been waiting to read this book. I also know that this is my creativity that I am experiencing because I have to write it, that I love the doing of it even though it is frequently painful, and that while I am writing it, I am in flow.

But I recently realized that while this book reflects some of my creativity, it has very little to do with my co-creating. One day, after writing for hours, I stepped into the shower, feeling productive and satisfied. As I was soaping my body, I asked my soul how it was doing (an exercise I recommend as part of being balanced and whole) and imagined what it would say to me. If souls could talk, mine would have answered: "I don't care." As soon as I realized this, I was shocked. My soul did not care at all about my writing, what I have always considered my creative outlet.

Instead it cared about my connection—to my Self and to others. It did not appreciate the many moments when I felt discouraged because the words would not flow. It hated when I denigrated myself because of my efforts. It intensely disliked my negative thoughts and feelings when the work was not going well. It was unhappiest when I was not available or loving in my interactions with those I most love. My soul was not at all interested in or impressed by my doing; its entire concern was for my being. It wanted me to become aware of how I was experiencing my Self in every moment, and it wanted me to experience myself as the best that I could be. I learned that day in the shower that co-creating is on a much higher creative plane than demonstrating artistic or literary creativity.

What is the lesson? A teaching story
Perhaps the simplest differentiation between creating and co-creating is that the former involves making something external to the self while the latter involves making the Self. This next story will not make sense from a purely

creative perspective, but it makes complete sense as soon as the concept of co-creating is applied. Remember, co-creating means to take complete responsibility for your Self and what you can control. You cannot control what the world does to you (and you are not responsible for what you cannot control), but you can control what you do with the world. And you owe it to yourself to remember who your partner in the co-creating process is and how much worth and meaning you yourself then have.

A LONG TIME AGO in a village built in a small clearing in the jungles of India, there was a huge cobra that was biting and killing the children of this village. This went on for a year and a half; many children were killed, and the villagers naturally were extremely upset by this situation. One day an itinerant monk came upon the desolate village and asked for food and shelter. The villagers agreed to his requests and told him their sad story of the dangerous snake. They asked him if he could help. They wanted to know if he had the power to speak to the snake and stop all the killings.

The monk, who was also a yogi, said he could speak with the snake. So he went into the jungle and called the cobra to him. The cobra appeared, rose up before him, and spread his hood in preparation for an attack. The monk was not afraid and asked the snake: "Can you imagine the karma that you are now creating for your next life?"

The surprised snake retreated from his attack and replied: "These children I have bitten are not innocent. They come looking for me, and when they find me, they taunt and tease me. I am acting only in self-defense."

After some discussion the yogi convinced the cobra to stop biting the children because of the bad karma that he was creating. He returned to the village and told the adults that he had spoken with the snake and their problems were over. He thanked them for their hospitality, they thanked him for his intervention, and he went on his way.

Several months passed. The yogi monk returned to the village and went in search of the snake. Eventually he found it lying on the ground with its skin torn, about to die. "What happened to you?" he asked the cobra. "You were so beautiful before. Why are you now ragged and dying?"

The snake replied with whispered voice: "You told me that I could no longer bite the children, so when they taunted me, I let them. This is what they have done to me."

The yogi laughed and gently touched the snake. "I told you not to bite them. I did not tell you not to hiss."

The degree to which I am authentic is
the degree to which I am spontaneous.

5

THE FIFTH STEP:
Spontaneity

MY EARLIEST MEMORY is of fear. Many years later I learned that this is normal; infants are born with fear, primarily the fear of abandonment. But what I remember was very personal and very scary. I thought that I was alone in my fear and that all those around me, who were big and strong and capable, were unafraid. At least that was my early perception. I was fearful of noises, of heights, of being hurt, and of being alone. I wanted to feel safe and secure and to have someone around all the time, someone taking care of me and stopping my fear. So I learned, before I could communicate, to please others, to be nice, to be "good." I was willing to pay any price not to feel afraid.

Without being aware of what I was doing, I set the wheels in motion for the next thirty years of my life and how I was going to respond to others. I desperately wanted to feel safe and secure, and I thought that I had found my safety; pleasing others would keep them near me, while asserting my true Self would drive them away. Being nice, doing what others wanted, was a lot of work, but not being nice, not always doing what they wanted, being real, would lead to my being alone and afraid again.

Several years ago, when recounting my early fears and my need to be nice instead of real, I was asked by my mentor, Buzz O'Connell, when had I changed. I could recall the exact moment for him. I was thirty, and I was driving in heavy fog. I could not see even the front of my car, to say nothing of the road. I was alone, and I was afraid. My hands hurt from gripping the steering wheel, and my eyes were strained from staring into the fog, trying to see through it. I was barely moving along the road, and I was already tired, even though it was early morning. To make matters worse, I was frustrated at my lack of progress and worried about being late for my first class. I became angry at myself for being afraid and also at the fog for being in my way.

All of a sudden I consciously let go. I stepped on the gas and began to speed along the road. I remember my revelation very clearly: Life is just like being in a fog; there are so many things that are out of my control, but I always have a choice. I can crawl along, scared, angry, and afraid of what is ahead, or I can let go and take my chances. I can still remember the feeling of exhilaration I experienced when I decided to take the risk. I liked myself better as soon as I decided to move. Paradoxically the fog began to lift as soon as I stopped fighting it.

The most amazing thing that happened that day was that as soon as I let go, I became a more spiritual person. That was the moment that I first lost my fear of dying and that I let go of my need to try to control everything. That was the moment that I stopped being so nice by always trying to please. Without fully recognizing what I was doing, I became real. From then on I practiced taking more risks and I started doing what I wanted to do, instead of always deferring to others. I went from being a frustrated phobic to a more spontaneous person, someone who could live life and enjoy it, who could face the unknown and perceive her problems as challenges. I became a pilgrim.

What is spontaneity?

One synonym for spontaneous is *instinctive;* this makes sense because being spontaneous means "acting in accordance with or resulting from a natural feeling, impulse, or tendency and without any constraint, effort, or premeditation." Whenever there is an external cause or influence, spontaneity is lost; it occurs only within its own energy or force. The definition that is probably most appropriate for this discussion is "self-acting." Having spontaneity simply means being in an authentic state or acting from free will.

Another way to describe it is "completely living in the moment." This idea may sound familiar—the here and the now—but it is usually quite difficult to achieve. This is because we are trained to consider what we are doing with respect to the past and, particularly in this culture, the future. We have learned to feel comfortable with guilt over the past and anxiety for the future; these act as constraints upon the present and prevent spontaneous behavior. How can we be spontaneous when we are worrying about what has already happened or what is yet to occur? Furthermore, whenever we worry about what others may think of us and what we are doing, we change the energy or force away from ourselves and give it to the others; we react rather than act. Spontaneity in these all too familiar situations becomes by definition impossible.

Moreover, when we are not comfortable with our concept of Self, it is again impossible to act from this foundation; we simply cannot be self-acting. In this case, we are acting with our facades, so carefully developed and presented by the weak ego. We may hold the delusion that we are choosing what we are doing, that we indeed are acting from free will, but this is yet another illusion of the ego. We are born spontaneous—instinctive—but as we develop, learn, and grow, we become programmed by our scripts (who we are as determined by others) and believe we must follow them in order to be effective in our many roles. In so doing, we lose the concept of being unified or balanced and instead perceive ourselves as compartmentalized and often fragmented role players.

To change this and become spontaneous again, we need to remember that we do indeed have free will; we can choose to be who we really are and how we manifest our Selves. This means that it is our responsibility to be the best that we can be, not for others but for ourselves. Also, because we are always changing, we will need to keep rediscovering who we really are; this is a lifetime process. Instead of allowing the externals—the world—to define and control us through our doing, we need to keep the focus on the internal Self, our being. Allowing ourselves to be spontaneous is one way in which to balance our doings with our beings; then we can be more fully alive and present in the moment.

Why is being so difficult?

The more involved we become in doing, the farther away we move from spontaneity or, in its essence, being. We have been taught always to be doing something and to feel guilty when we are not active. We have been trained to worry constantly about the future and to value tomorrow over today. Given these circumstances, it is easy to understand why we cannot stop and allow ourselves to experience the moment. And why now is not a comfortable concept. It is easier to let our minds, under the influence of our egos, keep driving us by focusing on what we will achieve or do next than it is to stop and become aware of who we are right now, how we feel, what we need, and what we have. Thus, our weak egos, fed by our insecurities, push and pull us out of the moment. Our minds, our emotions, and even our bodies are pressured into trying to live in a time frame—either the past or the present—over which we have no control. Ironically, we then find it difficult to live in the one time frame over which we do have control: this moment.

The soul is spontaneous. It experiences without judgment each moment. But we cannot become aware of these experiences when we are involved in the frenzy of living out of time. The awareness of the Self cannot occur in the activity of doing; this can happen only in the stillness of being. Best-selling author Neale Donald Walsch explains this very clearly: "Enlightenment is understanding that there is nowhere to go, nothing to do, and nobody you have to be except exactly who you're being right now. You are on a journey to nowhere. Heaven is nowhere . . . now . . . here."

Why is spontaneity a virtue?

To become truly spontaneous, we need to learn to deal with life as death. In other words, we become aware that everything around us is always changing and that every experience we have, every relationship, and every encounter are time-limited. All these things will end, and we will always be involved in the process of grief and loss. The degree of fear that we have toward change is exactly the degree to which we lack spontaneity, for to be spontaneous is to be open to the ideas that life is temporary and that everything around us is constantly transforming.

The virtue of spontaneity is that it directly relates to our ability to let go. The soul knows that this ability is critical to being; the ego fights this with all its force, knowing that the ultimate letting go is of the ego itself. Ultimately the ego will die when the soul reconnects to the Whole. We cannot become one with God and still retain our separate (and separating) ego. Therefore, we can recognize the similarity between the loss of a loved one and the death of the ego. In the former we are forced to let go of another; in the latter we are letting go of who we think we are and accepting who we really are—our true Selves. Being spontaneous can be thought of as practicing for this ego death, for when we are being our Selves, we are not under the influence of the ego. The more we let go, the more we have spontaneity. And the more spontaneous we become, the easier letting go becomes.

But how can we be happy or content amid all this change and death? How can we become spontaneous when we are so afraid of loss and pain? How do we begin to stop being influenced by the externals and start being influenced by our internal Selves? We begin, as we do in all endeavors, slowly and with small steps. We begin by realizing that every moment is precious, and it is such because it is temporary and will not last. Thus, it is important to appreciate each moment for what it is and who we are in it, rather than to want it or ourselves to be something or somewhere else. Next, we begin to see the mystical and mysterious, which exist all around us. We actively and openly search for the wonder, the unknown, the new. We open ourselves to the total experience of the now, and we experiment by seeing things through different eyes. In effect, we are closing the ego's eyes and opening the eyes of our souls.

And finally, we hope. Hope is one of the cardinal virtues, and it may be one of the loveliest and most powerful of all. It requires risk, trust, reliance, and the belief that what is wanted will occur. As the French novelist Georges Bernanos once said, "Hope is a risk that must be run."

Above all, hope is desire accompanied by anticipation or expectation. Again from Neale Walsch: "Desire is the beginning of all creation. It is the first thought. It is a grand feeling within the Soul."

To be spontaneous means to be instinctive; this is exemplified by being real or authentic. Being real means living in reality, and it is realistic both to be aware of the wonder of the moment and to be hopeful. The highest hope we can have is to have meaning or, in short, to be connected to the ultimate reality. As soon as we experience our Selves as part of it all, we yearn (hope) to be one with it all. This is our most spontaneous experience, our most instinctive journey, the end of our pilgrimage.

What is the relationship between spontaneity and religion?

Acting spontaneously requires authenticity; being authentic means being open to the Self as it exists right now and, at the same time, understanding that this will change. We cannot control the evolution of the Self any more than we can control the world. We cannot create a constant or fixed Self, just as we cannot create our goodness. This is because goodness is innate; it comes from God and reflects God within us. We can, however, encourage and live this goodness, thereby creating ourselves in the image of God and discovering that who we really are is found when we are spontaneously being our true Selves.

This is not the traditional teaching of many religions.

Some try to convince us that we are innately bad and must redeem ourselves through their practices. Others tell us that we must constantly monitor our thoughts, feelings, words, and deeds and watch that we behave appropriately. All religions have some type of catechism to determine virtue. Usually these involve religious obligations, such as going to church, tithing, and following the rules or strictures of each denomination. All preach the need to be honest, kind, moral, correct, and charitable. However, instead of functioning as guides along the path to enlightenment, many religions act as dictatorships—sometimes benevolent, sometimes not—in their need to control the behavior of their followers. The very nature of organized religion is in direct opposition to freedom of choice, the concept of free will. Thus, religion itself can create fear, guilt, and anxiety, rather than teach us to remedy our own insecurities.

Fundamentalists and zealots of all denominations are alike in their fear of spontaneous behavior. Their main concerns are power and control, the very antitheses of spontaneity. Following the rules, as they define them, is mandatory; following the true Self, believing in innate goodness, and acting instinctively are unheard of. Usually these dictators of virtue fail to recognize that we as humans contain God just as God contains us; together we are involved in creating and creation. And that this is a spontaneous process, one that is ongoing, ever-changing, flexible, and transformational, known and mysterious at the same time.

As soon as any group becomes a formal organized structure, by definition it stops being spontaneous. The concept of organization—becoming organized—is the opposite of the concept of spontaneity—being instinctive. There is nothing wrong with becoming organized; in fact, it is a necessary prerequisite for learning, working, living, and achieving effectively. It is a critical part of doing. What is wrong is that the equally critical aspect of being, as reflected in the concept of spontaneity, is ignored or denigrated. We need the balance between doing and being, organization and spontaneity, in order to become whole, real, and enlightened.

Being religious often means following a specific organization's beliefs; being spiritual means believing in the true Self and trying to follow the soul. Any religion that demands mindless (and soulless) compliance with its rules, that tries to control behavior by punishment, that threatens dire consequences (hell) for disobedience, and that does not recognize the power and beauty of the individual human spirit will not encourage virtue but will instead stifle its development. On the other hand, any religion that rewards spontaneity, that believes in the discovery of the true Self, and that recognizes that the pilgrimage to the soul is a personal and individual journey with its own timing and development will function to encourage the discovery of the soul. It is extremely difficult to undertake a pilgrimage all by oneself; however, if we are being discouraged by others, it is preferable to go alone. The very best we can hope for is to be surrounded by traveling companions who are supportive, loving, and encouraging (giving us courage).

What is time out of time?

Compared with Western religion and philosophy, the Eastern traditions seem to be more aware of spontaneity as a virtue. Perhaps this is because they are older, perhaps because they are wiser, but most probably because they are a reflection and a manifestation of their cultures. The East is, and always has been, more interested in the idea of simply being; the West is, and always has been, more preoccupied with doing and achievement. Zen captures in a very simple and concise description the entire essence of spontaneity: Between thought and action there is no judgment. For Buddhists, an important goal is to accept every moment completely. Every experience, no matter how small, is perceived as connected to and reflected by an enduring power. In order to reach this stage of enlightenment, one must transcend the opposites and move past the limitations of right and wrong, good and bad, time and eternity. The latter is relevant to the virtue of spontaneity, for it involves both living in the moment and being out of time.

In our more scientific Western culture this experience is

known as flow and has been investigated as a critical component to creativity. The poet Mark Strand describes what flow feels like: "Well, you're right in the work, you lose your sense of time, you're completely enraptured . . . caught up in what you're doing. . . . The idea is to be so . . . saturated with it that there is no future or past, it's just an extended present in which you're . . . making meaning. It's meaning carried to a high order. It's not just essential communication, daily communication; it's total communication." What he is describing is being so completely in the moment that one transcends the concept of time.

This seemingly contradictory experience is hard to comprehend with our singular concept of time. The Greeks solve this contradiction by having two words to define time, each with a very distinct meaning. *Kronos* is measured time, our typical perception of time as chronological—seconds, minutes, hours, years, and so on. *Kairos,* on the other hand, is participation in time or timeless time. This occurs when we become so engrossed that we lose track of chronological time—this is what is meant by being out of time—and it is perceived as the higher form of the two, for it is both renewing and nurturing. This is the time that is essential for being. Here is when we become one with the Self and the soul; here is when everything becomes connected. Our life—our time—is not linear or measured; it does not move in an orderly, progressive direction toward a fixed spot. Instead, as Einstein discovered, it turns and bends back on itself; it comes full circle. This is what the Self must do to experience that there is a center and in this center, all things are one.

Zen author Frederick Frank has discussed his experience of discovering the center: "Then I heard the falling of the snow, with the softest, hissing sound. I stood transfixed, listening . . . and knew what can never be expressed: that the natural is supernatural, and that I am the eye that hears and the ear that sees. And what is outside happens in me, that outside and inside are unseparated." I have had similar experiences in my own life; they are rare and very special and usually concern being in nature. Once I was sitting in a forest, waiting for a companion to compose a photograph. I remember that I stopped thinking about how much time this was taking. I let go and just allowed myself to be in those beautiful surroundings. All of a sudden I clearly and loudly heard water running; a stream on the other side of the mountain, which I could not see and was not aware existed, began singing to me. I became one with the stream, the trees, the mountain itself. I remember feeling pure, blessed, and very peaceful. But the most powerful recollection I have is the utter feeling of bliss: Nothing was wrong; nothing was out of place; everything made perfect sense.

What is one path to spontaneity?
Nowhere is this concept of being in time dealt with as completely as in the philosophy/religion of Taoism. Theo-

logian Huston Smith describes Tao as "a testament to man's at-home-ness in the Universe." The philosophy behind it is simple: Get the foundations of your life—your Self—in tune with Tao, and then allow your behavior to flow spontaneously. This means that first you must discover who you are in accordance with the Tao (the right path) and only then do you act. Action follows being; stronger and wiser action follows stronger and wiser being. This creates a circle to the center, a circle in which the action and the being are one. The goal of Tao is to let the Tao flow in and out of you until all life becomes a balanced, unrestricted pattern of harmony without any tension. No motion is wasted; no moment is ignored.

Most important, there is no concern with external appearances or outward show. This uninterest in the externals of life, the things that the world values and seeks, is profound to the Taoist. The core of this philosophy is that the harmony, the balance, the peace that men yearn for can be found only in the inner Self. Lao-tzu wrote the *Tao-te ching* (the Taoist Bible) in short verses. Similar to the teaching stories, the meaning of Taoism is not always clearly revealed but must be searched for and thought through. The following verse demonstrates the essence of Taoist philosophy; the five colors, tones, and tastes represent the sum total of our worldly desires:

> *The five colors can blind,*
> *The five tones deafen,*

The five tastes cloy,
The race, the hunt, can drive men mad
And their booty leave them no peace.
Therefore a sensible man
Prefers the inner to the outer eye.

What is the connection among spontaneity, self, and ego?

Carl Jung conceptualized the Self as the midpoint between the ego and the unconscious, related to both yet equivalent to neither. He perceived it as the source of energy that urges the person to become what one is. For Jung, it is an archetype that provides a sense of order and meaning in the personality, and it is the ultimate goal of psychic development. Jung's Western psychological concept of the Self is remarkably similar to the Eastern Tao. Both Jung and the Tao see this Self as beyond definition or description yet as the center of meaning, the source of grace in the moment, the connection to that which is eternal. This Self is our internal experience of relationship with the Whole. In effect, it is our soul; it is what connects us to God and to all things. Simply, it is being who we really are, and this requires spontaneity.

We all are familiar with the experience of two related things occurring at the same time. Our rational scientific minds label these as co-occurring incidences, coincidences. But both Jung and the Tao view these things as more than that. The Tao perceives them as evidence of the underlying connective principle; Jung calls them synchronicity. This is the link between two connected and meaningful events that cannot be explained simply as cause and effect. Synchronicity can occur between a feeling and an event, a dream and an event, or a premonition and a future event. In all cases there must be meaning between the Self and the event, and the Self must be open to the idea that it is meaningfully connected and related to the Whole.

This openness to connection cannot occur when the ego is in command, for the ego perceives the self as separate and isolated, logical and linear, limited and time-bounded. Instead, when the ego rejects any connection to the larger Self, what results, according to the author and psychologist Jean Bolen, can be compared with "living in a disordered country." This is a perfect description of what happens to those who become lost in their egos. I have seen many clients who enter therapy in this condition, and they indeed look just like refugees: confused, frustrated, helpless, vulnerable, and sometimes numb. However, often they deny just how disordered they are, for their egos are still trying to preserve their facades. So they come to therapy as refugees come to a new country—not because they want to change but because they have no choices left. Life is forcing them to go to a new place. Some of them are driven by their anxieties and fears while others demonstrate aggression and hostility; all try to blame the world for their conditions. Their egos have become insatiable, and there is simply not enough in the world to satisfy them any longer. As a result, they can never enjoy what they have, they can never relax and be in the moment, they can never, as Alcoholics Anonymous says, "Let go and let God."

Unfortunately this may sound all too familiar, for we clearly live in an ego-controlled culture, one that reinforces the development of the individuated, aggressive, and strongly separated ego-self. It is no accident that in this state we describe ourselves as alienated from the world; what we have become are aliens from God's connection, our state of grace.

Why does the ego fear spontaneity?
The foundation of the ego is fear. The first fear is that we will not survive, and in order to ensure our survival, we attach to others so that they will take care of us. While this attachment from fear is necessary for the infant and child, it becomes debilitating for the adult. The cost for continuing to attach to others because we are afraid is too high; at some point in our development we need to discover that we can survive on our own. By the time we are ready to make this discovery, the ego has become entrenched in our self-perceptions and does not easily give up its power over us. Having been nurtured by all our insecurities, it has become a dominant voice, much louder than the voice of our souls.

The ego's primary purpose is to retain our separateness,

our "me-ness." In order to be effective, it must appear to be strong, powerful, right, and in control even though it never escapes from its foundation, its fear. Thus, it creates a dilemma for itself: It must appear to others to be what it wants to be, rather than what it really is. To admit weakness, to expose insecurity, to be wrong are death to the ego, and this it must resist. The reality of the ego, a reality it cannot admit, is that it is an illusion, fostered by other illusions, a delusion that creates a delusory world, an external facade designed to keep others away from the internal reality, and the exact opposite of free will or spontaneous choice. Because its focus is upon the external world—what others think, how things appear, what is possessed—it must react to the world rather than act upon the world. Thus, the ego—the fear—produces the energy that runs away, closes down, protects by hiding or harming, judges, separates, and limits.

The true Self is just the opposite. Its foundation is love, and it produces the energy that confronts, expands, shares and heals, seeks similarities, connects, and moves past the boundaries. The evolution of the true Self begins when the fear—the ego—is confronted and the insecurities are allayed. This work only occurs internally; the external world cannot help us in this critical pilgrimage to the soul. Instead the world will usually seduce us and keep us from taking the journey. The ego pushes us out into the world to find meaning, and it uses fear as the motivator. The soul pulls us inside to discover our true Selves; its motivator is love and acceptance. The ultimate choice, our exercise of free will, is whether we live in fear (controlled by the ego) or whether we live in love and discover our true Selves.

Best-selling author Neale Walsch captures this concept most elegantly: "Every action taken by humans is based in love or fear—every single free choice you ever undertake arises out of one of the only two possible thoughts there are: a thought of love or a thought of fear. . . . You have no choice about this, because there is nothing else from which to choose. But you have free choice about which of these to select."

Spontaneity occurs when we act in accordance with a natural feeling and without any constraints. The nature of fear is to constrain us and cause us to react. When we are afraid, we are genetically programmed to flee or to fight. In either case, we do not usually feel that we are choosing our behavior but instead feel overwhelmed by our fear. It takes a great deal of courage and desire to override fear and conditioning. It is not easy to replace fear with love; it is very difficult to move past the separate and vulnerable ego state to the connected and accepting soul.

Author and therapist Rollo May addresses this issue: "In human beings, courage is necessary to make being and becoming possible. An assertion of self, a commitment, is essential if the self is to have any reality. . . . A man or a woman becomes fully human only by his or her choices and his or her commitment to them. People attain worth and dignity by the multitude of decisions they make from day to day." The Self is found not in the large and important acts of our lives but in the everyday actions we choose. Who we are determines how we act, and how we act reinforces who we are. Surely this is the message at the heart of all religions, the lesson that Christ, Muhammed, Gandhi, Buddha, Martin Luther King, Stephen Biko, and countless other enlightened ones have made so clear in their lives and words. It is not enough to wait for the big events or dramas to demonstrate that we can confront fear (violence) with love (acceptance). In order to be real, in order to be who we really are, we must consistently in all our actions choose connection over separation, relationships over power, giving over getting, acting over reacting—in short, the Self over the ego. Ultimately this becomes the only choice we have.

How can I be both spontaneous and responsible?
Eastern philosophies view life as a series of developing stages with each stage having a different but equally important role in your growth. The purpose of youth is simply to learn, the purpose of the householder (adult) is to involve and share the self with family, profession, and community, and the purpose of retirement is the opportunity to learn again, but this time to gain an understanding of life before you leave it. These stages imply that life is change and that change is natural. In other words, you are going to be in different places with different goals de-

pending upon your age. Therefore, what is instinctive at one age will not be at another. At any given time you are in your own stage; spontaneity requires acceptance that where you are is exactly where you need to be. You simply cannot compare your journey with anyone else's. Instead you must accept that who you are, what you are doing, and where you are going are your own personal pilgrimage. And this is how it should be.

The concept of karma takes this idea one step farther: Each individual, so the Hindus believe, is wholly responsible for his present condition and will have exactly the future that he is now creating. This belief is precisely the reason that spontaneity is a virtue rather than merely an instinctive action. You now know that being spontaneous means being yourself, but you also need to realize that as an adult with free will you are completely responsible for your being. It is not enough to act indiscriminately just because you feel like it; you must act purposefully with recognition that there are always consequences. And yet, how can you act purposefully and spontaneously at the same time? The only answer to this is that your spontaneity must be a reflection of your best Self and not a manifestation of your base self, your ego.

Remember, spontaneity is derived from an energy or force within. This is the key to identifying which part of you is creating your behavior. It is true that your ego resides within you (it is after all your creation), but its primary concern is what is outside you. Therefore, the ego is energized by and responds to your external world. Because it is the manifestation of your fears and insecurities, it usually chooses to react rather than to act. When your ego is in control, your seemingly spontaneous behavior is actually controlled by an external source. When your true Self, founded in love and energized by your internal being, is dominant, your behavior will be both spontaneous and responsible. It will be a manifestation of who you really are at this stage in your life and what you are going toward in the next. Not only will you be controlling yourself in the present, but you will also be creating the future that you deserve, the future that your soul wants to experience.

How do I practice spontaneity?

Given all that you now know about spontaneity, this question may sound contradictory, for how can spontaneity be developed if it is an instinctive, unconstrained activity? Again, you must go back to the idea of choice, that you alone have free will and can choose how to be. In the preceding pages it often has been said that your goodness is given, but your choice to live your goodness is not predetermined. Spontaneity is a virtue, not because it is instinctive and therefore uncontrolled but because it reflects the nature and the state of the person. It is a manifestation of the true Self, a perceivable and real force, something that can be seen, heard, felt, and touched, one of the ways that the mystery of God within can be observed and known. When you demonstrate spontaneity, you are showing the world your inner being, your reality, your connection to the Whole.

All this sounds daunting and impossible only when your ego is dominant. In order to restrain your ego and allow your true Self to appear, you can do some simple exercises that will hasten your progress. Each night you can take an inventory of what you said and did that day. Find something, just one thing, about how you acted that you do not like, something that makes you feel uncomfortable or defensive. Do not give in to your ego, and start justifying or making excuses for your action. Instead identify which part of you—your ego or your true Self—was responsible for your behavior. (A hint: If you are not at peace with what you did, it will usually concern your ego.)

Now start thinking of alternative things that you could have done or said. Play them through; pretend that you did each one, and imagine what could have happened. Again, question the source, ego or Self, of each alternative. Finally, select the action that makes you feel the best about yourself and rehearse it several times. Granted, this is not spontaneous behavior, but it will lead to such. The next time you are in a similar situation, if you take a moment to remember what you have done, you will find it easier to choose the behavior that reflects your true Self. With very little practice, you will spontaneously act in accordance with yourself. The importance of this exercise is that it teaches you how to constrain your ego; it helps you recognize that you have other choices.

Another very simple exercise is to tell yourself that you love your Self before you begin any difficult interaction or endeavor. This stops your ego cold in its tracks. Any rebuttal to the simple statement "I love myself" is the ego talking, and what it says can be ignored. The more you do this exercise, the easier it becomes and the more natural and right it feels. Say it often; say it even if you don't believe it or mean it. Say it because you know you need to; say it because you know you want to; say it because you hope that one day you truly will. Take the risk; say the words "I love my Self." Why shouldn't you? It is indeed a wondrous and glorious Self; after all, it is part of God.

A third exercise can be called getting in touch with your internal world. Begin by asking your soul what matters. At first you probably will not get a response, but keep asking. The soul is aching to be heard; it cannot wait to respond, but its voice is very quiet and requires great stillness in order to be heard. It is this stillness that your ego most fears, so your ego will create noise. It will use your mind to create thoughts, your emotions to create feelings, your body to create aches and pains. Become aware of how the ego operates, and it will begin to lose its power over you. Treat it as a pet monkey; tell it "Enough is enough." Restrain it, laugh at it, ignore it, but do not fight with it, for then it will always win. Keep on asking your soul what matters, what is important. One day it will tell you, and you will know that your pilgrimage is successful. You are on the right path.

Finally, recognize that the true Self is the same self in all situations and under any conditions. When you can be the very same person from the beginning of the day until the end of your night, when nothing else or no one else causes you to change from who you really are, then you have found yourself. This Self has no roles to play, no need to impress, no face to save, no facade to protect. This Self is real and strong, certain only of itself, in control and fearless, not of the world but of who it is and why it is. As the poet e. e. cummings stated, "To be nobody-but-your-self—in a world which is doing its best, night and day, to make you everybody else—means to fight the hardest battle which any human being can fight; and never stop fighting." This is the pilgrim's quest and ultimate goal.

What is the lesson? A teaching story

This is one of my favorite teaching stories because it can be applied to many situations and a wide variety of problems. It is especially useful in times of great anxiety or misery, and it never fails to bring a quick smile of recognition in times of great joy. I use it here to exemplify the virtue of spontaneity that requires the awareness that time is both limited and changing and that no matter how hard we try, we cannot control it. Once we recognize this and let go of our expectations, illusions, and attachments, we can truly live the moment.

ONCE UPON A TIME in a far-off land there lived a wealthy and powerful king. He had one beautiful daughter, and he desired her to marry well. He summoned many princes from surrounding countries to interview with his daughter. The princess, although beautiful and kind, had a serious problem. Whenever it was time to meet the princes, either she would burst into convulsive laughter and laugh her way through the interview, or she would burst into tears and tragically cry until the candidates left. This behavior, hysterically laughing or crying, continued for several months and caused all who met her to reject her. (Nowadays we would give her a diagnostic label and try to medicate her condition, but back then these options were unheard of.)

The king was becoming exceedingly frustrated by her behavior and worried that he was running out of eligible princes. Finally, in desperation, he called together his group of twelve wise men and issued this edict: "You have twenty-four hours to come up with a solution that will stop the princess from laughing hysterically or crying profusely. If you do not come up with the right answer, all of you will be beheaded." Upon saying this, he threw the twelve wise men into a dungeon and left them to deliberate.

Eleven of the wise men huddled together and moaned and groaned about their upcoming fate. They agreed that there probably was no answer to the question of what would make one stop being happy or sad. Instead they chose to bewail their doom. The twelfth wise man sat off by himself all day and all night and pondered the problem. The next day, at the appointed hour, the king called the wise men to his chambers and asked them if they had a solution. Eleven of the wise men began making excuses and begging him to spare their lives. The twelfth man stepped forward and said: "There is an answer to what will make one happy when one is sad and what will make one sad when one is happy. I have engraved this answer inside this gold ring." He handed the ring to the king, who held it up to the light and read: "This too Shall Pass."

The degree to which I am appreciative
is the degree to which I am generous.

6

THE SIXTH STEP:
Generosity

It WAS NEARLY Christmas, always a stressful time of year, and it was early morning—the worst time of day for me. In my haste and typical blurry confusion of the first hour after awakening, I almost missed what Catherine was up to. She was six years old, a first grader, and as usual, she was scurrying out the door to catch her school bus. I instinctively knew that today, however, something was different, so I looked at her closely. She had on her coat—that was good. She was wearing warm clothes, gloves, boots, and a hat—also good. And then I saw it.

"Whoa," I cried, stopping her at the door. "What do you have in your satchel?" First graders are not typically laden with many heavy books, yet her book bag was straining at the seams and required both her tiny hands to hold it.

Catherine looked guilty and obviously wanted to escape quickly from me. She shuffled her feet and said, "Oh, Mom, I gotta go or I'll miss the bus."

"You are not leaving until I see what is in your bag."

Reluctantly and very carefully, she put down the satchel and slowly, oh, so slowly, began to open it. I looked down and was shocked. For there, sitting in her bag, carefully surrounded by her papers and books, was her ceramic piggy bank.

"Catherine! Why in the world are you taking this to school? Is it for show-and-tell?"

She shook her head and looked as if she were about to cry. "No, Mom. I'm going to give it to Tony."

"What?" I'm afraid I yelled at her. "But this contains all the money you've been saving all your life. All the money that your grandmas and your aunts and uncles and the tooth fairy and Daddy and I have given you since you were born is in this piggy bank. I thought you were saving it for something important, something you really wanted and needed one day."

We were not an affluent family. We always had to be careful with money. Birthdays and Christmases always involved choices for the girls. They could not get everything they wanted, so they had to choose what they most wanted. There was always something they were dying to have, and it took great strength for Catherine not to have broken into her piggy bank many times in the past. And yet, here she was, wanting to give it all away.

"Tell me what is going on." I pulled her inside the house and unzipped her jacket. "Don't worry about the bus; I'll drive you to school. Now sit down and tell me what has happened." I suspected the worst; I feared that she had broken something of Tony's or perhaps was being intimidated by him and trying to buy him off. You never know what is going on in the battleground called childhood.

"Well . . ." she tentatively began. "Yesterday we were sitting in our circle on the floor, and the teacher asked us what we were getting from Santa Claus. Everybody said something—I said I was getting a Barbie doll house—and then Tony said that he wasn't getting anything. The teacher asked him why not? Had he been a bad boy? Tony said: 'No, ma'am. My parents told me that we were too poor for Santa to come to our house.' And then, Mom, he started to cry. So last night when I was in bed, I thought about it. I thought that if I gave him my money, then he would not be poor and Santa could come. If Santa still didn't come, then he could buy something he wanted with the money. Mom, please don't be mad at me." She started to cry.

I was overwhelmed. And I was very proud. Here, on this normal day, in my home, sitting before me and shining out at me, was one of the purest examples of a loving heart. At six years old, my daughter was teaching me the beauty and joy of generosity. She was giving because she wanted to; she was sharing because it made her feel good. And, paradoxically, she was also afraid that she was doing something wrong. Of course, in a way she could not possibly understand, she was. She could not solve Tony's problems; she could not make Santa come to his house; she could not see that giving money could be embarrassing to both Tony and his family. She knew only that she wanted to share her wealth; she wanted to share what she had with another. In her purity, in her desire to give of herself, she was truly beautiful.

What is generosity?

We know, of course, that generosity reflects the quality of being *generous,* which means "being willing to give or share, being unselfish, or being magnanimous." "Being bountiful" and "being liberal" are also meanings of *generosity,* although not as commonly used. But perhaps we are not as familiar with the origin of the word *generous.* Initially it described a person of noble birth, hence, nobleminded; *generosity* then meant "nobility of mind." This archaic definition is the best beginning to the discovery of this virtue because it takes us back to our beginnings— where we came from and who we really are. It is a more complicated concept than simply the idea of giving, which usually refers to giving away external things. We are taught that we are generous if we give anything at all; therefore, it is quite easy to give things that have little value to us in order to feel rewarded by our generosity.

But if we conceptualize generosity as nobility of mind, we come closer to what being generous really entails. And once we can perceive ourselves as created in the image of God or being part of the Ultimate Creator, we can understand that all of us, all living things, are of noble birth. Despite our external situations or physical manifestations (our life roles), all of us have the potential for nobility. It is inherent in our relationship to our greatest Lord, the highest Prince, the King of all. When our thoughts and our actions reflect this ancestry—our inherent nobility or innate goodness—then our minds are indeed noble, and we are, by the original definition, generous.

Why is generosity a virtue?

The relationship between this characteristic and the cardinal virtue of charity is very clear. *Charity* also means "benevolence," "almsgiving," "altruism," "humanitarianism," or most simply "the luxury of doing good." However, the descriptions for *charity* go further than the definitions of generosity; they include tolerance, goodwill, brotherly love, acceptance, patience, understanding, and openheartedness. In order best to comprehend the value of this virtue and to understand how we can demonstrate it in our lives, we need to perceive the virtue of generosity as it is related to our minds and our hearts. Thus, it becomes a reflection of our being both noble-minded and openhearted; it is indeed a balance between our rational minds and our empathetic hearts.

It is, like all the other virtues, a paradox and not as simple as we may first believe. The virtue of generosity is not found just in what we give or when we give it; this is merely what we do. Instead its virtue is found in who we are, our being. The highest or purest manifestation of this virtue is found only when we give ourselves, and the value of this gift lies in the perception that we hold of our own worth. If what we give has little or no value to us, we are not being virtuous in the giving. We are merely getting rid of useless or extra "stuff." It is too easy to clean out the closets of our lives and give away what is unwanted or outgrown; it is far more difficult, and therefore virtuous, to give what we love and cherish. The ultimate gift, then, is to hold ourselves in high esteem and give ourselves away.

To accomplish this seemingly contradictory task, we must understand exactly what we are giving; we must recognize the value of our gift. And this requires appreciation, which I perceive as an essential part of, perhaps even the foundation for, generosity. To appreciate something requires that we hold it in high regard; we think well of it, we value it, we are grateful for it, and we are fully and sensitively aware of what it means to us. For when we appreciate something, we feel grateful; we *give* thanks. The German mystic Meister Eckhart revealed the importance of this: "If the only prayer you say in your whole life is *Thank you*, that would suffice."

What is one path to generosity?

All six of the major religious traditions are similar in what they give us. All supply ethical guidelines, all promote the concept of virtue, and all provide us with some vision of a spiritual reality. While all religions stress the virtue of charity, perhaps the best example of how it can be manifested in everyday life is found in Islam. The term *Islam* is derived from the word *salaam*, which means both "peace" and "surrender." The essence of Islam, its purpose and quest, is to find the peace that comes only from surrendering one's life to God. For Muslims, this surrender is manifested in both submission to God and charity to their fellowman. The submission is active and real; it is demonstrated five times each day in their prostrating themselves on the ground and offering a prayer of praise, supplication, and appreciation. Theologian and author Huston Smith says this prayer is offered "in response to the natural yearning of the human heart to pour forth its love and gratitude towards its creator."

This daily prayer ritual is the second pillar of Islam; the first is to verbalize at least once in a lifetime that there is no God but Allah, and Muhammed is His prophet. The fourth pillar is to observe Ramadan, a month of fasting, and the fifth one is to make a pilgrimage to Mecca, if at all possible. But it is the third pillar that is germane to this discussion, for this is the stipulation that "Those who have much should help lift the burden of those who are less fortunate." Any follower of Islam who has material holdings and money must give a specified percentage to those in direst need. This is distinct from the practice of tithing, used to support the church, or charity as one chooses; this is a required and honored sharing of wealth as part of one's submission to God. For Muslims, God is honored through the giving of oneself—the submission—and by the charity to one's fellowman—the sharing.

Furthermore, Islam asks its adherents to view the world as the brotherhood of man. This translates into absolute racial equality—intermarriage is not only allowed but was often demonstrated by their prophets—and complete acceptance of other religions. The Koran is specific on this point: "Unto you your religion, and unto me my religion." Thus, the open-mindedness and openheartedness that define generosity are stressed as central to the practice and beliefs of Muslims. This acceptance of others and the recognition that we all are brothers under the skin are the higher form of charity, for they entail both generosity of faith and generosity of spirit.

What is the nature of generosity?

We have learned that it is easier to find pleasure in things that are easy to obtain—things external to ourselves—than it is to find pleasure in ourselves. Therefore, it makes sense that it is also easier to give away external things than it is to give away the Self. The easiest giving of all, the one we often use to satisfy our charitable needs or obligations, is to give external things that we have grown tired of or will no longer miss. This type of charity is not the virtue of generosity. The virtue of giving is found in following our true natures; we give because we want to give, we give because we want to be of service or to make a contribution or to help ease suffering. The highest form of giving occurs when we are able to give of ourselves without any expectations of return or reward. The very best we can ever offer is our truth, the way we truly are. We realize this only when we undertake our internal journey—our pilgrimage to the soul.

There is an ancient Chinese proverb that says: Tell me

and I will forget. Show me and I may remember. But involve me and I will understand. This involvement with another is the most difficult of the three gifts because it requires time and the giving of the Self. To care enough about someone else to become involved with him, to accept the place he is in without judgment, to value your own knowledge and to recognize your ability to teach—all these are manifestations of the true nature of giving. Teaching a starving man how to fish is a far more generous act than throwing that same man a fish.

The later teachings of Lao-tzu, founder of Tao, are explicit in this regard: "Suppose a person amasses a worldly treasure and then gives it all away to those in need . . . [and suppose another person] cherishes these teachings [the Tao] and uses [them] to instruct others and serve them selflessly, the blessings of this person will be far greater than those of the former . . . for the one who practices Tao and then guides others gives spontaneously whatever he has, simply because it is his nature to do so."

We give because we cannot *not* give, just as we take because we cannot *not* take. An analogy to this is breathing: We take a breath and we are taking in; we release the breath and we are giving out. This is a spontaneous and unconscious activity, a requirement for life. When we become aware of what we are doing, we learn to control the process and allow our breath to be mindful and to work for us. We learn to use our breath to help us relax, still the mind, calm the body, and allow us to contemplate, meditate, and observe without action. We learn to use this natural and normal process to help us get in touch with our internal being and connect to the greater Whole. In much the same way, we can become mindful of our giving natures and use this awareness to enhance our self-worth and increase our connection to others and, through them, to God.

Why is the ego not generous?
If giving is indeed as natural as breathing, why, then, is generosity a virtue and part of the pilgrimage to the soul? The answer is once again found in the ego. It is simply not in the ego's nature to be generous, for it is too busy counting, weighing, measuring, and comparing. Its purpose, remember, is to separate us from others and to create an illusion of safety for our comfort. In order to accomplish these objectives, it cannot risk losing any part of itself or its attachments. For the ego, existence is determined by what it possesses, whom it controls, and how well it can protect itself from the unknown. Thus, the only way that the ego knows to give is to barter: "If I give this, what will I get back?"

The concept of giving—either giving in or giving of one's self—is literally death to the ego, for nothing will be left if everything is given away. To the ego, nothing is more important than preserving and maintaining the separate self. Every activity is directed toward confirming the need to be individual and special; the only actions that count are those that will benefit the ego. Taking in, then, becomes far more critical than giving out. By its very nature, the ego is stingy; nothing is enough, and giving to others means that we will have less. Remember, to the ego, our worth depends upon what we have—not on who we are. This is the root of much of our human misery.

Why, then, do so many of us succumb to the ego? The answer is found in our development: We begin our lives by attaching, first to our mothers and then to others who care about us. Because it takes many years and a great deal of wisdom and maturity to discover that our true Selves cannot be attached to anything except our souls (which are attached only to God), we begin by associating our attachments to others and to external things as necessary for our survival. Because of this association, we believe that our egos—our separate selves, our me-ness—are who we are. The ego and the me—the image presented to the world—become stronger and stronger until we completely lose the awareness that we have any other self. This is how it is for most of us, so this must be how it is meant to be.

It is only when we become mature enough to survive on our own that we become ready to detach from the ego and reattach to the true Self. By the time we are ready to begin this work, our egos have become firmly entrenched in our beings and, to make matters worse, reinforced by the external world. The ego's view is unfortunately society's perspective. Thus, we will not get much help from the external world, which supports attachment to the ego, to begin our detachment from it; therefore, we must undertake a personal pilgrimage in order to find the true Self.

What is the ego's game?

If we do not do this internal work, we get caught up in the ego's game. Part of this game involves identifying with our external roles and dichotomous perceptions. We begin to see everything in terms of opposites: If I need to see myself as a healer, then I need to see you as sick. If I need to be helpful, then you must be helpless. If I perceive myself as giving, then you must be perceived as taking. If I give you something, then you must give me something of equal or greater value. American psychologist and Indian philosopher Ram Dass describes this process: "If everybody gets caught in your ego game—you lose. And if you win and find your ego's security, you end up alone in a prison of your own making—and again you lose. That's the horror of the ego game: If you win, you lose."

In order to avoid this game, it is necessary to understand why the ego's attachment conflicts with the Self's generosity. The ego comes from fear; the Self comes from love. The distinction between the two is made evident by author Neale Donald Walsch: "Fear wraps our bodies in clothing, love allows us to stand naked. Fear clings to and clutches all we have, love gives all that we have away. Fear holds close, love holds dear. Fear grasps, love lets go. Fear rankles, love soothes. Fear attacks, love amends." To live in fear, to exist in the ego's domain, means that you cannot allow your generous and openhearted nature, your love, to show. You must constantly remain on guard and aware of what others are doing, what they are taking from you, and what you are lacking. In short, you must remain attached and vigilant until finally you become paranoid.

Why does generosity require non-attachment?
Zen, as usual, answers this question in one simple sentence: "To give is non-attachment; that is, just not to attach to anything is to give." Attachment to something prevents us from revealing our true natures, our generous and loving Selves. This relationship between giving, loving, and detaching is made explicit by Swami Vivekananda: "Work and expect nothing in return. Work because you love the world. Then you can unattach—become free. [When] everything given by you is a free offering to the world without any thought of return, then your work will bring you no attachment. Attachment comes only where we expect a return." In short, the virtue of giving lies in the wanting to give of one's Self and not in the blessings one receives from the giving. Whenever we start to be concerned about receiving rewards or appreciation from our charity, we are no longer demonstrating the virtue of generosity.

One example of giving without attachment is to give something—a present, your time, a kindness, or a favor—anonymously; then your pleasure is in the pure act of giving. Another example is to ask the receiver what he would most like you to give, and even though it may be something you would never choose, give it because it is for him, not for you. But the best example of all is to give something and immediately forget that you have done so, for the best gifts we give are often unintentional or unremembered. In other words, remove all the hoopla from the gift process. The act of giving is your reward; the gift itself is irrelevant. What the receiver does with your gift is also irrelevant—to you, the giver.

What is being described is one form of unconditional love, love without attachments. Whenever we hold expectations or conditions, the gifts we give are no longer pure, spontaneous gestures from our hearts. They are instead gifts with strings, and there is a price for the recipient to pay. Often this price is worth more than the gift; this is not generosity but often thievery because the expectations of the giver are usually not made explicit. Nobody wins in this exchange because the gift is not really a gift at all. This is the ego's paradox because, as the social philosopher Eric Hoffer revealed, "There is a sublime thieving in all giving. Someone gives us all he has and we are his."

What is the paradox of generosity?

Once we can subdue the ego—detach from its controlling influence—we quickly discover the paradox of generosity: The more we give, the more we have, and what we have is bliss. For there is no distinction between giving and loving; our joy on this earth is found in the love that we give.

It is precisely in our ability to give of ourselves that we are able to transform ourselves into that which we most yearn to be, who we truly are. Author and scholar Joseph Campbell described this process: "When we quit thinking primarily about ourselves and our own self-preservation [the ego's domain], we undergo a truly heroic transformation of consciousness. . . . [Usually] we're so engaged in doing things to achieve purposes of outer value that we forget the inner value, the rapture that is associated with being alive, is what it is all about. . . . [However,] if you follow your bliss, you put yourself on a kind of track, which has been there all the while waiting for you, and the life that you ought to be living is the one you are living."

In some form or another, all religions teach us that every act of love brings happiness. What is real, what matters, what brings us joy are found when we comprehend the connection among living, loving, and giving, when we see that all three are aspects of being the One. Then everything we do reflects who we are. Our giving is tied up in our loving, and both are simply part of our being. As Mahatma Gandhi said, "My life is my message." Every act that we do, even every thought that we have become part of the pattern that determines the quality of our lives. As soon as we see that our generosity toward others is really only our giving to ourselves, we discover the bliss. Then we give because there is nothing else we can do; we give because we love, and what we love is the God we see inside ourselves and inside all living things. Every act that we do, once we are transformed, eases the suffering because our intentions are pure.

Gandhi also described this awareness: "There comes a time when an individual becomes irresistible and his or her action becomes all-pervasive in its effect. This comes when the person reduces himself to zero." What is being reduced to zero is not the true Self but the ego, for it is only the ego that stops transformation. It is the ego that prevents the natural generosity of spirit; it is the ego that stops the purity, the naturalness, the inherent goodness from being acted upon. Therefore, it is only the ego that keeps us out of joy.

The Zen Buddhist concept of satori transcends the distinctions between self and object and self and other. In achieving this transcendence, Zen Buddhists believe, one sees that the world is overwhelmingly beautiful, there is goodness in all, and the welfare of others becomes as important as one's own well-being. Once we reach this stage, we experience as much joy for another's good fortune as we do for our own. In so doing, we in turn receive all the blessings that life bestows. These blessings, the bliss are not found outside our everyday lives but are embedded in the very ordinariness of everyday activity—in our work and our routine behaviors. Thus, we do not have to change everything in order to feel the joy or receive the blessings; we only have to subdue our egos (a formidable task!) and allow our true Selves to surface. Then we will see that "All is one" and that the Divine exists in the ordinary. A good illustration of this comes from author Huston Smith's translation from the Chinese:

> *My daily activities are not different,*
> *Only I am naturally in harmony with them.*
> *Taking nothing, renouncing nothing,*
> *In every circumstance no hindrance, no conflict . . .*
> *Drawing water, carrying firewood,*
> *This is supernatural power, this marvelous activity.*

A shorter quotation from Blaise Pascal sums it up: "The power of man's virtue should not be measured by his special efforts, but by his ordinary doings." But how do we transcend, how do we transform, how do we find the bliss in our everyday activities, the same activities that cause us so much stress and strife? How do we give without attachment? How do we love unconditionally?

How can I balance my head with my heart?
A good friend of mine recently returned from a monastic retreat. She told me that over and over again the teachers on this retreat stressed that the longest and the most difficult journey that you will ever take is the one from your head to your heart. Your head contains what the world has taught you and therefore is usually controlled by your ego. Your heart, on the other hand, contains the love you feel

and therefore is more connected to your soul. Your Self is found in the balance between these two.

When you move past your ego and find the balance between the head and the heart, you will discover compassion, what the Buddhists call karuna. It is composed of both the love of man (the heart) and the awareness of his suffering (the head); it is not at all sentimental or condescending, but it is very painful. It is said that you can see the smile of unbearable suffering in the Buddha's image. To see this, to remain open to the pain, is a requirement for becoming compassionate. It means that you have moved past your own fears and pains; in short, you have subdued your ego and are open to the pain of the world. You have done what Mother Teresa recommended: "Love until it hurts. Real love is always painful and hurts; then it is real and pure." However, if you only remain totally immersed in the suffering and the pain, you will eventually become attached to it or you will drown in it; in short, you yourself will become an object of pity.

In order to remain compassionate, you must find the balance; you must "walk a tightrope of action without attachment." To do this, you will need to recognize that there is a master plan, a lawful order, and that everything on one level is as it should be. While you cannot completely comprehend the perfection of this world, the reasons that things are as they are, you can use this awareness to alleviate the suffering and the pain. Your mind can comprehend that there is a greater purpose to what is occurring than you can know. But if you remain in the mental domain too long, if you find too much comfort in the fact that you cannot change the world, then your heart will harden to the suffering, and you will no longer feel empathy.

Mother Teresa's treatment for the lepers of India is a perfect example of the dual nature of compassion. This saintly woman wasted no time blaming the condition of the poor and sick on the government of India or the caste system or anything else. Instead she was both practical and nurturing. She did what she could do, and she founded a clinic to take care of the sick and dying. Because of her faith, she understood that everything in life has purpose and that there are reasons for suffering beyond our comprehension. This philosophy allowed her heart to remain open and loving without becoming immersed in the pain.

We too can practice finding the balance between our heads and our hearts; if we can avoid becoming stuck in either place, eventually we will be able to be in both at the same time. This place is the balance between the two; this means that we simultaneously comprehend the overall pattern and keep an open heart. To do this is to live in paradox: We live in the reality that we cannot change the world yet will still do our best to ease the suffering.

This is a very difficult task, but this is what is required by the virtue of generosity. As Confucius said, "Virtue is mail. teamblackbear.com

125hbb

Ctme e tbb

200 Capitol 100

barbar @ teamblackbear.com

bbHthelper1

The 5 Value Propositions of Keller Williams

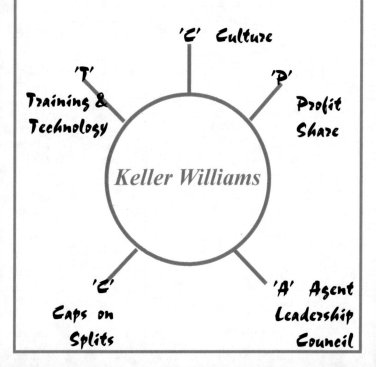

'C' Culture

'T' Training & Technology

'P' Profit Share

Keller Williams

'C' Caps on Splits

'A' Agent Leadership Council

to love men." The Talmud tells us that the highest wisdom is loving-kindness. Yet to live in love is very difficult, and to make matters worse, not all others will understand and receive your gift of compassionate love in the same spirit in which you give it. To cite Albert Schweitzer, "Anyone who proposes to do good must not expect people to roll stones out of his way, but must accept his lot calmly, even if they roll a few more on it."

To make it even more complicated, you need to distinguish generosity from the idea of sacrifice. The virtue of generosity is not the same as self-sacrifice, for once you feel that you are sacrificing yourself, you are again vulnerable to your ego. If you think that compassion simply means to serve or be helpful, you begin to perceive what you are giving in terms of what you are doing and the roles that you and the other are playing. The way to avoid this ego game is described by Zen author Laurence Boldt: "Buddha asks: Who are you helping with your helping? Everyone is already the Buddha. Therefore, it is silly to get serious about helping and to think you are saving others."

How can I live in the balance?

The psychologist-turned-guru Ram Dass tells of the trips he once made to Benares, India. The first time he went, he felt guilty because he had only traveler's checks and no coins to give the beggars. The next time he went, he made sure that he had plenty of coins for them. He felt great pity for the dying poor and handed out as much money as he could. Then he began to look into their eyes, and he was surprised to see pity for him reflected in the beggars' eyes. He finally realized that they were feeling sorry for him; he was wandering all over the world looking for himself. They knew who they were and where they were. In this interaction lives the balance, the ability to see past the roles, beyond the externals and to perceive the true Selves inside all others with the eyes of your own true Self, and, above all, to try to ease the suffering without pitying or denigrating the other.

In order to live in this balance, you first need to recognize that everything you do can be an act of generosity, that your very being in this moment can be an example of love in action. As the seventeenth-century writer La Rochefoucauld said, "Nothing is so contagious as an example. We never do great good or great evil without bringing out more of the same on the part of others." It is important to realize that what you do in this moment, the generosity you show, will change both you and your world. Finding the balance, living the love, giving from your heart are the goals of your soul, for it desires both to experience the world and to give the world the experience of yourself. From this experience come the true meaning of life, your true happiness, and your real rewards. "For what shall it profit a man, if he shall gain the whole world, and lose his own soul?" (Mark 8:36).

How do I practice generosity?

Surely by now it is evident that the secret to practicing generosity is to be able to recognize the source of your giving. You need to know what is controlling your behavior: your ego or your heart? One simple exercise is to ask yourself before you act, "Where is this coming from? Is it my ego driving my behavior, or is it my loving heart? Am I giving to fulfill an obligation or to get something back? Am I giving because I need to be of service? Am I taking on the martyr's role? Am I giving now so that I can feel good later?" If any of these are the reason, the ego is in control. It is quite simple to determine when the heart is behind the action: You give because you want to, and there is no attachment to either the gift or the consequences. Thus, you give without regard for the action of giving. In other words, you give naturally and spontaneously because it is who you are; your action merely reflects your being.

Once you have identified the source of your giving, you can actively try to increase your truly generous actions and decrease the ego-attached ones. Stop giving gifts that have strings attached to them. Stop perceiving yourself in a role, and even more difficult, stop seeing others in roles. In other words, you are not the giver and they the takers, but both of you are part of the giving and receiving cycle of love. In order to find bliss, you must give, and in order to give, you need someone to take your gift. Therefore, the recipient is necessary for your happiness. Also, practice seeing with your heart's eyes; diligently seek out the beings inside all others. To do this, it helps to separate their actions from their true Selves; then you can judge their ego actions and still love their beings. Learn to resist giving to their egos, just as you resist giving in to your own ego. Give from love to love, and know that the greatest reward of giving love lies in the ability to love. Thus, the greatest gift, the highest form of the virtue of generosity—the soul's path—is found only when you both love your Self and give yourself to all that you love.

The other activity you can practice is to become more appreciative. It is not coincidence that the more you are grateful, the more generous you become. Appreciation means that you are actively aware of the gift of the moment and that you recognize the greatness of this gift by giving thanks. Stephen Levine tells the story of the wise man who holds up a glass in order to answer the question of how to live with an unattached heart—to live in compassion—when the world is ever-changing and constantly causing loss and grief. "See this glass. I see it as already broken. While I have it, I will drink from it, use it and enjoy it. When it breaks, which it will—ah, so! Of course." In this manner you learn to view everything—yourself, your loved ones, all living things—as temporary and in the process of dying. Then you can appreciate them while you have them. Then it becomes easy to see what you have right now and to give thanks for the great gifts you have. It is from this appreciation, this recognition of love, that your generosity will flow.

What is the lesson? A teaching story

The message in this story is not difficult to comprehend, although the story itself may be difficult for those of us reared in the West to relate to. We have been taught to fear death and to perceive it as an ending to all life, rather than a beginning of another type of life, as the Eastern philosophies believe. The reason I chose this story to exemplify generosity is that it is a paradoxical example of the nature of this virtue: We are only as generous as we are appreciative. Once we can get past the ego's greedy eyes and see with the soul's grateful ones, we discover that there is something to be thankful for in every moment of our lives. This story is also a good example of spontaneity because the relationship between these two virtues is strong.

ONE DAY IN the jungles of India a man was out walking alone. Suddenly he heard a mighty roar behind him, and turning, he saw a huge tiger bearing down upon him. He started running for his life and kept on running, just steps ahead of the tiger and imminent and painful death. After a few moments he came to a precipice in the jungle, and he knew he had to make a terrible choice. He could either jump to his death or face it in the mouth of the tiger. Instantly he chose to jump and flung himself over the steep cliff. As he was falling, he happened to notice a vine growing on the side of the precipice. He reached out, grabbed the vine, and clung to it for dear life. After a minute he caught his breath and began to feel hopeful until he realized that the roots of the vine were slowly giving way. His weight was pulling the roots out of the cliff. He hastily looked around for something else to grab, but all he could see was a single small plant containing one beautiful, large, succulent wild strawberry. With all his effort, he reached over and plucked the strawberry. He popped it into his mouth just as he felt the vine give way. His last word: "Delicious!"

The degree to which I love others
is the degree to which I love God.

7

THE SEVENTH STEP:
Spirituality

I HAD JUST ARRIVED in Madrid from Houston, and as usual, I was jet-lagged and exhausted. Even though it was early in the morning, I showered and went to bed, thinking how delightful it was to be in my good friend Elizabeth's beautiful house in a city I dearly love. I quickly fell asleep and was almost immediately transported into the most unusual dream that I have ever had. In this dream I was standing in a tunnel in the corner of a curve, so that I could see both where the tunnel started and where it ended. I was pressed closely against the wall, and my hands could feel its surface very clearly. It did not feel like anything I had ever felt before, yet what I was feeling was familiar and real. Immediately I knew exactly where I was, and I knew why I was there.

I was in the tunnel that is the passageway from this life to the next; I was looking into the afterlife and observing the light at the end of the tunnel. I was not in the least afraid; I knew with absolute clarity that I was not the traveler but merely an observer and that was why I was pressed against the wall. I could also clearly see God waiting just inside the light, and I knew that He knew I was there watching and that was how it was supposed to be. No words were spoken between us.

Then I looked to the other end and was very surprised to see a friend of mine entering the tunnel, and he also did not seem in the least afraid. I knew that he was not aware that I was in the tunnel. My friend quickly walked up to God and turned to him. In a gentle but strong voice, God asked him, "How do you think you are doing in your life? What do you feel good about?"

My friend answered, "I think I am a good man, a fair and just man. I try to be helpful and of service to others. I usually put those that I love or feel a sense of duty toward above myself and try to take care of their needs. I always try to be a nice guy."

"That is exactly the problem," God said, and then he started to yell at him. "You are nice instead of being real. You allow others to take away your spirit and to walk all over your soul. Don't you know that I have given you a light and this light is Me? You have almost allowed someone else to extinguish your light. You do not fight to protect it, nor do you honor it and recognize its value. You do not take care of the part of Me that is inside you."

God's eyes blazed. He shook his finger at my friend, and He stamped his feet. "You have almost let my light go out. Don't you know that people who have extinguished their lights try very hard to put out the lights inside others? Your lifework is to keep that light alive and to help others do the same with their lights."

And then I woke up. I was absolutely wide-awake, and I no longer felt any symptoms of jet lag. I was completely present in the room, and I was sitting up in bed. And I was awed, for this was an experience like no other dream I have ever had. This felt more real than the reality I saw around me. Every part of my body, all of my senses, re-tained this experience. My hands could still feel that tun-nel wall; my eyes could still see God, the light, the tunnel, and my friend. My ears could hear the voices, and my mind remembered every word precisely as it had been spoken. My heart was racing, and my head was reeling; I was feeling amazed, humbled, and awed at the same time. I knew I had been somewhere important and experienced something profound.

Later on, when I recounted this dream to my friend, we both intuitively knew that it was not a foreboding of his death but rather an answer for his life. He was dealing with a difficult decision, and this dream gave him a clear answer. Both of us knew that we had been given an un-derstanding of the purpose of it all, a deeper comprehen-sion of the meaning of life.

What is spirituality?

There are many descriptions of that which is spiritual, including that which is holy, sacred, or devotional, that which is concerned with the higher part of the mind and shows much refinement of thought and feeling, and that which is spirit or soul, as distinguished from the body. The *spirit* is defined as the "life principle"; it also refers to the thinking, motivating, and feeling part of a human. Thus *spirituality* refers to the "spiritual quality, character-istic, or nature of the thing, as opposed to the sensual or worldly one." Another definition is the "state of being incorporeal," meaning without material body or substance. To simplify, spirituality is the quality of being actively aware of and connected to the other reality, the one that is not of this material world or, from my dream experience, the light that is God.

To be spiritual, then, can be conceptualized as living in that light. It is interesting that this is referred to as the higher part of the mind; it is strongly related to the soul, which has been described as the ultimate thinking, feeling, and motivating part of us. However, this cannot mean that all our thoughts, feelings, and motivations are spiritual or soulful because by definition there is a distinction between the material world and the mysterious one. Therefore, whenever we are concerned only with the external world—the so-called real world—we are not practicing spirituality. To the enlightened, there is no distinction between these two worlds, as there are no polarities. But to the rest of us, this distinction is important because it will actually guide us toward our enlightenment, our being in the light.

My friend Judy spent a month in a monastery learning how to become more spiritual. I asked her what that meant, and she told me that spirituality requires community. We become spiritual beings when we simultaneously practice the commandments to love God and love our neighbors; we do not separate the two. Spirituality, then, is the demonstration of our love of God through others. It is experienced and made manifest in our interactions and relationships with others, rather than alone by ourselves. Perhaps this is what is meant by a Living God; surely it is the path to our bliss. As the medieval nun Julian of Norwich said, "The fullness of joy is to behold God in everything." Community requires sharing, which is really the purpose of all relationships, and in sharing, we find both our happiness and our meaning. In order to experience life, we must interact and interrelate; in short, we must connect. We simply cannot experience the light within ourselves—immanent God—without sharing this experience with others. We also cannot experience the beauty in the world—transcendent God—until we can see the light in all creatures. In order to do this, we need community.

Perhaps the clearest description of spirituality is that it is how the soul reveals itself, and the vehicle it uses is relationship. This idea is remarkably similar to the pioneering psychiatrist Alfred Adler's concept of social interest: Once we develop self-esteem, then we naturally care about and share with others. My mentor, Buzz O'Connell, says that self-esteem (actively loving the Self) and spirituality are equivalent and part of the same process because both spontaneously lead to our ultimate commitment to help others develop and expand themselves. Therefore, finding the true Self is the same as discovering the spirit. Both processes create and increase encouragement—the giving of courage and love. In short, the more we love ourselves, the more we love others. The more we love others, the more we love God. And, to make the circle complete, the more we love God, the more we love ourselves and all others.

Why is spirituality a virtue?

Of all the virtues we have encountered along this pilgrimage, this final one is the most self-evident. After all, our entire quest is a spiritual one; what we are seeking is the soul, and we find it as soon as we uncover the true Self, our spirits. Spirituality is also the characteristic that has the most obvious relationship to a cardinal virtue, for having spirituality is another way of describing having faith, which simply means believing or wanting to believe in God. It is nearly impossible to conceptualize spirituality without a Higher Power or a unifying force greater than that which we can see. God is mystery. He has to be; He cannot be scientifically proven. We have to take a leap of faith when we believe. As I learned in my childhood, to those who believe, there is no question; to those who do not, there is no answer. This is why being spiritual—believing what we cannot comprehend, living what we cannot know, and encouraging what cannot be made tangible—is virtue.

We know that virtue is goodness, and we also know, because our goodness is innate, that we do not have to believe, we do not have to have faith, in order to be good. We are good; we do not have to do anything to create this goodness. But what my dream made evident to me was that we do have to protect our innate goodness, for this is the light that God gave each of us. It is possible to protect this light without believing in a Higher Power; in order to do so, we have only to believe in innate goodness. If we do not believe in this, if we do not have this as our foundation, we will inevitably extinguish the light. Moreover, once we have lost the light within—the reality of our own goodness—it is a natural progression to convince others that they also are not good. It takes a great deal of work and energy to become truly evil, rather than merely misguided. Perhaps the above is the true meaning of evil: the process of deliberately eliminating the light. Unfortunately this phenomenon is quite common.

Why do we need evil?

Evil exists, and like goodness, it is contagious. One of the questions that has plagued mankind from the beginning is how can a benevolent God allow evil to exist. The only probable answer to this may be found by understanding the concepts of experience and free will. In order to experience something and be aware of what we are experiencing, we must have an awareness of what that experience is and what it is not. Otherwise the experience has no meaning, for it cannot be defined or described. We understand doing only in relation to not doing; we comprehend living only because of dying; we become aware of what is good only when we have knowledge of what is evil. Remove the evil, and there exists no possibility for understanding the concept of goodness. Everything would be equal, and goodness as we know it would not exist.

We are taught that God granted us free will; this means that we are given choices. In order to choose, we must have a selection of things from which to choose. In short, we must have opposites, polarities, dichotomies. If God had created the world and not allowed evil to exist, there would be no choices to make. There would be no right or wrong, good or bad, black or white. Then we would not have free will; this would be a meaningless concept, for everyone would be good, everything would be right, and there would be no possibility of experiencing anything. We would not be human beings with the potential to enhance our lives and become enlightened; rather, we would be mere puppets or playthings of some Higher Power. We would lose the opportunity for pilgrimage, for there would be no journey to take, no capacity to experience ourselves, and no need to learn from our experiences.

Instead we are blessed because we are allowed—no, more than that, we are required—to make choices. We have been given permission to experience evil (to eat the apple) in order that we may choose goodness. We have been given the choice to believe or not to believe in a Supreme Being, for without that choice, free will would be a hollow mockery. And what is even more incredible, we have been assured time and time again that God's love is unconditional, without any conditions at all. This means that we are loved even when we do not love back; we are loved even when we choose not to believe. Incredibly we are loved even when we choose evil over goodness! Therefore, it is completely in our hands whom we choose to become; it is entirely our responsibility to protect the light within or to extinguish it. For no matter what we choose, no matter what we do, God loves us.

All this is exactly what virtue is all about. It is a choice we must make, and we do so not to receive God's love, for that is already given, but to experience that love for our Selves. We choose to be virtuous simply because it is what we want to be; in so doing, we choose to become co-creators with God. This means that we take on the responsibility for ourselves, including our spirits and souls, and we open ourselves to the pain and suffering that are inherent in these responsibilities. We choose to make our lives mysterious, challenging, difficult, and painful so that we may experience what God is experiencing. Unconditional love means letting go with an open heart. There is no more difficult path; there is nothing that is harder to do. Because it is so difficult, God allows us to choose it, not for Him but for our souls. The all-knowing soul understands that virtue is the harder path, but the soul also knows, as the French essayist Michel Montaigne said, "I walk firmer and more securely uphill than down."

Why is virtue always paradox?

It is known that all great truth and all religion is paradox; similarly, virtue is also paradox, for that which tries to comprehend the mystery by definition must be inconsistent with common experience and full of contradictions. Becoming virtuous is also paradox; as Lao-tzu explained: "Superior virtue is not intentionally virtuous, and thus is virtue. Inferior virtue does not let go of being virtuous, and thus is not virtue." In other words, doing the right thing because you want to be correct or giving in order to get something back is not real virtue. Perhaps Confucius explained this best: "The superior man loves his soul, the inferior man loves his property." Superior virtue, then, is any action coming from the soul while inferior virtue is somehow involved with external appearances, the ego.

The paradox of the virtue of spirituality is that we must try to live what we cannot know; we simply lack the depth of mind to be able to comprehend the Whole. The best we can do is take leaps of faith and realize that we will never "know" the whole truth. Paradoxically, the more caught up we get in trying to fathom the truth, the less spiritual we become. Medieval mystic Julian of Norwich explains: "The more we busy ourselves to know God's secrets, the further away from the knowledge we shall be."

However, spirituality requires that we *experience* God within ourselves and *perceive* God in all others. We must experience what cannot be completely known. And we must do this for ourselves and in the ordinary reality of our everyday lives, which are not conducive to this task. In short, there is no recipe or formula for becoming spiritual. There cannot be because this is an individual process; it occurs as soon as we become aware of our true Selves. Looking for the way takes us away from the process. It is the difference between reading a cookbook and getting in the kitchen and cooking.

All the virtues that we have encountered are paradoxical; they have to be in order to be virtue. The paradox of objectivity is found in the requirement that we see ourselves as we really are, but in order for us to make this observation, we need to distance from ourselves. We must create a space away from ourselves in order to see inside our Selves. In other words, we cannot know our Selves from the inside out; we must start from the outside in, yet we cannot discover our internal worlds by using the external world. If this isn't paradox, what is? The paradox of integrity is just as difficult. The virtue of integrity comes from pure intentions but not from intent. In other words, we do not demonstrate integrity when we are consciously trying to do so. If we think that what we are doing reveals this virtue, it does not; then we are operating from ego. In short, the true Self does not see integrity in any particular activity or feeling; our integrity is inherent in who we are and not what we do, although what we do is part of who we are.

Morality is not any easier. Often we will lose our moral

reputation when practicing this virtue, for reputation is based on the world's perception of what is good. The virtue of morality requires that we live our own truth—our innate goodness—and this often means breaking the external rules. The paradox of spontaneity is that it is grounded in self-discipline; the true Self is both instinctive and disciplined. Spontaneity is not the same thing as impulsivity; the latter means that the ego is demanding action, while the former means that the true Self is acting. To understand the paradox of creativity, we simply need to become aware that while the world honors and encourages the creation of the ego and its creations, only the soul understands the creation of the Self, and only God fully perceives co-creation. The paradoxical quality of generosity may be the easiest to understand: Sometimes the most generous act of all is not to give but to allow the other to discover.

Paradox turns the world upside down. It keeps things interesting and mysterious. Virtue also changes the world, but in a more personal manner. It means that we go inside in order to live outside. It requires that we go down to the depths so that we may rise to the heights. It is the process in which we lose all sense of meaning (the ego and the world's reality) in order to find real meaning. We must lose part of ourselves in order to discover our complete Selves. We learn to love ourselves, give to ourselves, and put ourselves first so that we may give to others, love and serve them. We begin the pilgrimage hoping to find ourselves, and what we find is that we have to let go of the baggage of our lives in order to discover who we really are. And what we discover is that our real Selves have always been there. We are not finding anything new; we are simply uncovering the old. When we think we know it all, we know nothing. When we know that we know nothing, we discover that the soul knows it all. We desperately seek meaning in our lives, we grasp at connection and belonging, and we are afraid of both finding and losing our deepest desires. All we really need to do is to let go; then we discover that what we most want we already have. There is nowhere for us to go to find the soul; thus, the pilgrimage is itself a paradox.

How does religion describe virtue?

All religious traditions agree that the purpose for our lives is to work out our salvation diligently and that the best way to do so is with humility, loving compassion, and faith. They all also agree that the stories of our lives are difficult ones, fraught with problems and suffering, but that it is our response to these hardships that gives us our characters. Life is difficult because it has to be. We are here to transcend the difficult, discover the important, go beyond the mundane. The goal of faith, according to theologian Huston Smith, is not altered states but altered traits. We are in search of not mysticism but awareness, and it is this that leads to changed behavior. The journey of religion is a journey to discover the spirit in the soul, and we discover it not in comfort and ease but in hardship and pain.

Each religion tells a part of the whole story exquisitely well. Every tradition has something important, something elegant and remarkable to add to the understanding of the mystery. Thus, we can think of every religion as contributing another chapter to the story, and similar to a good mystery, each tradition gives us an important clue that points us toward the solution. Each of them can help us in our journey to God, but none of them can reveal God personally for each of us. Rather, they are "fingers pointing to the moon"; they can show us the direction, but they cannot make us take the journey.

Understanding virtue is simply another finger pointing to God. All religions deal with all concepts of virtue, but I have arbitrarily chosen a specific tradition to exemplify each of the seven modern virtues presented in this book. From Hinduism's four wants and two paths of life, we can learn to accept who we are and where we are; when we can accept ourselves as we are, we become objective. Buddhism gives us a precise description of integrity, how to get it and how to live it, in the Eightfold Path. Confucianism explains the importance of morality as the foundation for the Self and the society. Taoism stresses the virtue of spontaneity—the true Self living in the moment—while Islam teaches us the actively consistent nature of generosity. Judaism, with its history of intimate and dynamic interactions with God, shows us that we are indeed co-creators of this world. Christianity provides us with still another means to understand the concept of living our goodness. It is important to recognize that all religions teach the need to love God and to love our fellowman; all traditions place the virtue of spirituality at their centers. I have chosen Christianity to exemplify spirituality not because it is the only path or necessarily the best path to this virtue but because it may be the simplest. For when asked to clarify his message, Jesus summed it all up with just one sentence: "Thou shalt love the Lord thy God with all thy heart, and with all thy soul, and with all thy strength, and with all thy mind; and thy neighbor as thyself" (Luke 10:27). And this love is the essence of spirituality.

What is one path to spirituality?

The two central premises of Christianity give us yet another understanding of our own natures and of how God perceives us. The first premise teaches us that we are all sinners; the second tells us that we must be broken before we can be one with God. The importance of the first premise lies in the recognition of our humanity: We are not perfect, and therefore we will sin. The revelation here is that God created us imperfect, and at the same time, He continually forgives us and loves us with all His being. This premise makes it very clear that we are not God. Yet we also are taught that we were created "in the image of God." German mystic Meister Eckhart explains this contradition: "God is in all things as being, as activity, as power but He is procreative in the soul alone; for though every creature is a vestige of God, the soul is the natural image of God." Since only our souls are made in the image of God, the rest of us reflects our own images. So because we are not God, we will sin, and because we are not God, we are forgiven and loved just as we are. In short, God does not expect us to be God.

However, God yearns for us to be One with Him. The story of the life and death of Jesus Christ provides us with yet another means for reconciliation, whether or not we are Christians. Thus, the second premise becomes a critical finger pointing toward an answer toward unification, for it tells us that we must be broken before we can become One with God. The popular author Scott Peck writes of this phenomenon: "Such breaking is actually symbolized in the services of the Christian churches when, at the central moment of the Communion ritual, the priest holds a piece of bread high over the altar and breaks it." When Christians celebrate the Eucharist, they are demonstrating the willingness to be broken. Peck continues: "We need these moments of breaking, when we come to realize that we are not okay, that we do not have it all together, that we are not perfect, that we are not without sin." In order to understand the relevance of this premise to our own personal journeys, we need to review briefly the story of Christ.

Jesus, like all other prophets, came into the world a

newborn baby. This means that he came into the world in a completely human form—vulnerable, helpless, and afraid. If we believe that Jesus is indeed the Son of God, then we need to ask: Why would God want to manifest Himself in such a fragile way? The only possible answer to this is that He loves us so much in our imperfect human form that He chose to assume this form as proof of His love for it. Jesus lived and developed exactly as we do: an infant, a child, an adolescent, and finally an adult. According to the Gospels, he acted very much like a normal man. In fact, in his lifetime he never confused himself with God the Father. Jesus was often sad and depressed, lonely and afraid, frustrated and confused. He had close and loving relationships, and he was clearly a sexual being. He also had times when he needed to be alone. We know that he experienced dark nights of the soul as well as moments of great transcendence. No matter how we construe him—as messiah or as prophet—his life is a model for all our lives. In short, as Scott Peck states, Jesus always presented himself as a real and remarkably human person. Then, if we believe that he is the Son of God, we must again ask: Why would God want to present Himself in such a dramatically human persona? The answer must be to make it easier for us to experience God.

The most incredible part of this story occurs when Jesus is in his early thirties. He is crucified. Why would God allow this undeniably good man to be tortured and to endure such a horrible death? The answer must lie in what this reveals to us; obviously God really wants us to understand the message of this dramatic act. The symbolism of the crucifixion is found in its dual message: One part is the going to the Divine; the other is the Divine coming to us.

Why must we be broken?

The entire symbology of Christ's being crucified—his human body being broken—before he could be united with God is a very important concept for us to understand, whether or not we are Christians. In order to comprehend the meaning behind the symbol, we need to ask ourselves: "What is the most human thing about us? What is it that separates us from God? What is it that makes us sin and choose evil over good? What part of us keeps us so wretchedly connected to the physical world and stops us from venturing into the spiritual one? What is it that we fight so hard to protect—from all others and especially from God's love? What is the part of us that chooses to live in fear rather than in love?" The answer to these questions is not the soul, for this we know is the part of us that is the image of God. The answer is also not our spirit or true Self because this is the part of us that is always seeking connection to God. Thus we do not need to break either our spirits or souls. The answer of course is our ego.

Perhaps we can also use the Holy Trinity—Father, Son, and Holy Ghost—as a symbol to help us understand the nature of our own personal trinity—soul, spirit, and ego.

If so, then God the Father can be represented by the soul; the symbolism here is obvious because of the concept of immanent God, the God within us. The Holy Spirit can be symbolic of our own spirits or the true Self. This also makes sense because the Holy Ghost is how God manifests His acts; our spirits are how we demonstrate, through our love and actions, our souls. Moreover, the Holy Spirit is created from the love of the Father for the Son and the love of the Son for the Father; thus it is formed in love. Likewise, our spirits are created from our love of God and our love of others; they too are formed in love. And this leaves the Son to symbolically represent the ego.

This concept is not literal; it is only symbolic and not meant to imply that Jesus is or means ego. In fact, it is very clear that He tried to live an egoless life. But it also seems apparent from His frustrations and His doubt at the very end of His life that Jesus, like all of us, was fully human. Like all of us, He possessed an ego. The fact that He was crucified represents in its most symbolic form the need for the ego to be broken. For if we believe that Jesus is the Messiah, then we need to ask: Why did God choose to break His human son in such a terrible manner? We need to recognize that the crucifixion must have been as painful for the Father as it was for the Son. For what can be more painful than allowing your beloved child to suffer? In what other manner could He give us such a powerful symbolic message of what we must do to be One with Him?

This idea of being broken is not unique to Christianity; in some variant it is found in all traditions. Every prophet, every saint, every holy man or woman—from Buddha, Krishna, Muhammed, Lao-tzu, Confucius to the Old Testament prophets to my favorite mystics, Eckhart, Julian, Catherine, and Teresa—every one has experienced times of great agony, suffering, and alienation, a breaking from this earthly world and its possessions. The critical realization in this message comes when we ask: What precisely is being broken? Once we ask this, the concept of breaking becomes more obvious, the meaning in the message becomes clearer. In order to be in union with God, we must break the ego. We must crucify this part of ourselves, and it will be painful.

What is the connection
between science and ego, religion and soul?
Before the seventeenth century religion was the central concept of life. All forms of creativity were associated with the Divine; nature, science, and religion were inseparable. But then Galileo said the earth revolved around the sun, the church went ballistic, and religion and science split into two separate disciplines. Science went out to make sense of the eternal world, and religion went in to explore the internal world, the soul. Each of these disciplines ig-

nored the other; science dismissed the importance of the God within, and religion forgot that half the Divine exists outside. It is only recently, because of quantum physics and relativity theory, that there has been some integration of the two. Western science is beginning to sound like religious mysticism in its concepts of the interrelationship of all phenomena, the unity of the universe, and the recognition that all of nature is dynamic.

Biologist Rupert Sheldrake equates our souls to the scientific concept of fields, for both are "invisible interconnections" that hold the whole together. His coauthor, theologian Matthew Fox, says: ". . . what I like about [the concept of] field is that it puts our souls outdoors again. . . . Soul is the energy we put out into the world and the universe . . . through compassion and interdependence: responding to each other's joy and pain, through healing and justice making. And a field is a place where things grow. It's a place of wandering and playing—for our souls."

To be human means that you have both a soul and an ego. The split between religion and science encouraged the split between soul and ego. When religion chose the internal domain and science the external one, science and ego became partners. (In fact, the term *ego* became identified with Freud's psychological description of the internal realm—id, ego, and superego—with the ego perceiving the external world and controlling the id. This more "scientific" definition actually helped confuse ego with self.)

Because science was interested, until recently, only in what could be measured and duplicated—the so-called real world—these criteria were used to distinguish reality from unreality. The ego loved this, for now the soul did not exist because it could not be seen. Even God could be questioned because He could not be proved. Thus, our internal world became irrelevant, and the external world became the only place in which to derive our meaning and our reality.

For four centuries the ego has ruled supreme over the soul in much the same way that science has ruled supreme over religion. It is no coincidence that Western society, based on scientific rationale, has been labeled egocentric and narcissistic. It is only in the last few decades that some integration has occurred and that the importance of soul has been rediscovered. However, the idea that the ego is the least meaningful and most problematic part of our being is still not widely recognized. Psychology has helped spread the illusion that the ego is the sun and we revolve around our egos, our manifested realities. Perhaps a better analogy is that soul is the gravitational field holding everything together, spirit is the sun giving off light, and the ego is a black hole in the solar system, trying to suck in the light. We know that black holes are energy turned against itself; they are strong magnetic forces that destroy everything that enters their paths. They make a remarkable metaphor for those who have lost their souls and are consumed by their insatiable and destructive egos. It is not enough that they have put out their own lights; now they must try to extinguish all light.

How does the ego interact with God?

We can easily recognize that the ego prevents us from being spiritual; it prevents us from being truly intimate with others, and it stops us from feeling close to God. (One way to think of the ego is as an acronym for *e*dging God *o*ut.) The most dramatic way it does this is to deny His existence because He is not "real" in a scientific or normal sense. When we use this as our justification for not believing, we have forgotten that this same criterion applies to our egos; they too cannot be seen as separate entities or as "real." But we know we have them; why, then, is it so hard to know that God exists? The difficulty here is that we usually confuse our egos with ourselves and are not aware that the ego, as popular author Marianne Williamson says, is only "the impostor within us." She also uses the term *ring of fire* to describe what we have to face when we confront "our demons, our wounds, our egos, the ways we have conceived to deny love."

If our souls are dominant enough to subdue the ego and allow us to take the first leap of faith, for that is what believing in God requires, then the ego will allow that God is something that exists outside us, something so grand, indefinable, unknowable, and unimaginable that we cannot possibly relate to Him. Thus, we may believe, but we are still distanced from His love. When we conceptualize God as a patriarchal authority figure, we begin to fear Him. If we believe that God is like the stern, autocratic, dissatisfied, judging, and forever disciplining father, we are naturally going to repress our true natures and run from His view. If we think that we can never satisfy this commanding and powerfully domineering parent figure, we are going to behave much like an abused child. We may run to Him in moments of crisis, but we will never trust Him. And we will be angry, frustrated, lonely, and afraid; in short, we will feel abandoned.

Our difficulty with the concept of a loving God, according to psychologist and author Walter "Buzz" O'Connell, is that our egos simply cannot trust authority figures that we cannot manipulate. The ego has learned to satisfy its needs through manipulation: we must work very hard to get what we want. If we want to be loved by God, we must do something to earn and deserve this love. This type of thinking gives us the illusion of control over the situation, for we can then control how much love we receive. If I want a lot of love, I can make that my priority; if I don't need so much, I don't have to work so hard at getting it. But God loves us unconditionally; therefore, we have absolutely no control over whether or not we are loved; the entire process is out of our hands. To the ego, this is frightening, for the ego loves control more than it wants uncontrollable love. As a matter of fact, the ego is absolutely terrified of that kind of intimacy for fear that it will get lost in it. And the truth of the matter is, it will!

When the ego controls our hearts, we become afraid of losing ourselves in love. When the ego controls our minds, we become dubious of anything that we cannot fully comprehend. As Oriental scholar R. H. Blyth explains, "The intellect can understand any part of a thing as a part, but not as a whole. It can understand anything which God is not." The ego requires certainty along with the illusion of control; it simply detests a mystery. It loves things to be black or white, good or bad, right or wrong. It wants concrete answers that make rational sense. The ego masquerades as a true scientist, but the spiritual world is not a scientific one. "Life is religiously ambiguous—it does not tell us what we want to know," explains theologian Huston Smith. "If life told us the answer, it would remove our freedom. The ambiguity dignifies us by forcing us to find our own answers." But the ego cannot tolerate such ambiguity, probably because it needs certainty and a sense of stability in order to thrive. It flounders and becomes defensive when it is unsure; it believes that uncertainty is weakness and instability is chaos.

Why does the ego sabotage the soul?
Quite simply the ego cannot stand the noncompetitive nature of the soul. It cannot understand the paradox of spirituality; the contradictions in the mystery confuse it. The concept of God being both immanent (inside) and transcendent (outside) at the same time causes the ego to become frustrated by the enigma of it all and to turn its

frustration into cynicism. Furthermore, the ego does not like the idea that God is perfect and man is imperfect; its competitive nature wants it to be the best, and here is the situation where it cannot win. So ego blames God for the way it is; it blames God for making us imperfect sinners. Never mind that God loves us as sinners; this the ego cannot comprehend because unconditional love is beyond its capability.

As the mystic nun Julian of Norwich explains, "Some of us believe that God is All-Power and can do all, and that God is All-Wisdom and knows how to do all. But that God is All-Love and wants to do all, here we restrain ourselves. And this ignorance hinders most of God's lovers, as I see it." It takes strong constraint of the ego to conceive of God as desperately yearning for our love and wanting to be One with us.

Yet when we think of parenting, we can better understand this in terms of our love for our children: We love them because we have created them; we love them because they are vulnerable and need us; we love them because they struggle to make sense of it all; mostly, we love them because it feels natural to do so. However, we usually cannot love them unconditionally, for our egos get in the way; we want something back for all our efforts and our love. We want them to behave, to respect us, to follow our leads, to love us, and to attest to our worth and meaning in this world.

God yearns for us without any ego attachment. He

yearns for us to love Him not for what that will do for Him but for what it will do for us. For in our love we can heal the wounds inflicted by our egos. In this love we can create heaven on earth for ourselves. Only in this love do we discover that God is inside us and outside us. Only then will we know that God has nowhere else to be but here with us all the time. Only then can we understand what the mystic Eckhart meant when he proclaimed: "God needs me as much as I need Him." For in order to love, there must be something to love.

Why is the ego afraid of love?

Now we can see how the ego prevents us from believing in and wholeheartedly loving God—the first half of spirituality—and how it also affects the second half of this virtue—loving others. In many of the same ways that we fear losing ourselves in God's love, we are afraid of true and lasting intimacy in our relationships. Loving others means becoming vulnerable to them, and this can be frightening. Loving others also means exposing ourselves to them and allowing them to see us as we really are. If we see ourselves only as our egos, then we believe that there is nothing worth loving inside our facades. On the other hand, if we see ourselves as part of God, then we are not afraid to allow others to know us as we really are. When we perceive God inside ourselves, we become able to see God inside others. Then, instead of ego looking at ego, we become soul looking at soul.

This is the miracle of relationships: We become open and available to others, and in so doing, we melt the defensive structure of the ego and allow the soul to be revealed. This is the death of the ego-self; therefore, the ego will resist this type of relationship with all its might. For above all, it wants to preserve itself, but as Joseph Campbell reminded us, "Self-preservation is only the second law of life. The first law is that you and the other are one."

In fact, however, most of our relationships have very little to do with love and a great deal to do with need. We want relationships so that we will not be lonely; the ego is terrified of being alone. We want them to feel better about ourselves; the ego uses the insecurities of others as a source for power and control. We believe that someone else will complete us and make us feel whole; the ego loves this delusion, but as soon as we start to connect and become intimate, we also begin to criticize and become distant. The well-known lecturer Ram Dass explains why: "When the fire of love gets hot, ego gets scared and pulls back . . . the ego burns, the soul does not." Remember, the ego's purpose is to separate, to protect our individuality and independence. The soul does the opposite; it strives for connection and union.

What is the reason for relationships?

There is really only one purpose for relationships: They allow us to awaken from the illusion of separation and to come into union in our everyday life. Perhaps they are best described as rehearsals for our ultimate relationship with God. The easiest way to find our souls is to have loving relationships because the soul reveals itself in the spirit and the spirit requires others in order to act. The experience of love requires more than one participant in order to grow. Yes, we can experience love for ourselves by ourselves, but we need others in order for this love to expand. As a matter of fact, it is impossible to be spiritual without involving others. The proof of the authentic mystical experience—communion with God—is that after one there is more empathy, concern, and responsibility for all mankind. In short, we cannot experience God and remain indifferent to others.

Once we experience our own souls, it is a natural progression to perceive the souls in others. Again, this process is paradox, for we cannot force our souls upon those who are not yet awake. And as my dream experience shows, we must protect our lights from those who would extinguish them. Therefore, loving others is not as simple as it sounds (or else we would all do it all the time!). We must strive to love as God does—unconditionally. This means we accept the reality of who others are choosing to be, and we must allow them their choices and their timing. We cannot force ourselves upon them or desperately seek to save them unless they ask for our help. We cannot preach, but we can teach, and the best way to teach is to serve as a role model of what unconditional love looks like. We can learn that the ego applies the conditions; therefore, subdue that sucker, and let go of all conditions. We can learn to love the being even when we detest the behavior.

The biggest impediment to all this love is fear, and there are many good reasons to be afraid in today's environment. There are those who would hurt us for no reason, would take everything we have without a moment's thought, and would care nothing for our pain. The danger has always existed; it is not new. Yet if we destroy others in order to save ourselves, we become part of the danger. But if we allow others to destroy us, we are not protecting the God within. It may help to remember that the least spiritual part of our beings is the physical, and its destruction is not equivalent to the destruction of the spirit. In order to release ourselves from the overwhelming fear of physical pain and destruction (inevitable no matter what we do), we need to practice seeing with our souls' eyes. In other words, look beyond your fear of them, look past their fear of you, and try to connect your spirits. Try a little kindness next time you are afraid. The smallest gesture of love can erase the largest amount of fear; a tiny bit of soul can overcome a huge amount of ego.

What does spirituality look like?

I was very blessed in my encounters with the virtue of spirituality. I was not looking for it, but it came to me from two unexpected sources. My first encounters occurred in my profession as a therapist, and they occurred in the strangest places: in mental hospitals and the county prison and in dealing with abusers. I discovered that as soon as my clients showed me their vulnerable places, their pains and their fears, the next thing I saw revealed was their souls. The very process of therapy is conducive to subduing the ego because the client is admitting that he doesn't know and needs help. Clients are usually so desperate and in so much pain that they are willing to allow their ego-built facades to break. Once this occurs, the soul emerges. And once I saw their souls, I had no choice but to love them. I fell in love with each and every client who ever allowed me to see past the ego and into the soul. This love has no resemblance to the earthly, physical, or needy emotion as we usually know it; this love is spiritual, all-encompassing and all-consuming. No matter what happened after this revelation, no matter what the outcome of therapy or what happens in my everyday life, whenever I remember their souls, I feel this love.

My second spiritual encounter lives right in my house. My husband, Timothy, is a lovely and lucky man. He loves me absolutely and completely, and he has since the very first moment we met. You might think that I am the fortunate one to be the recipient of all this love, and I do indeed feel blessed. But early on, when I was not sure of the depth of my feelings for him, I realized that his ability to love was his gift from God and that he was the happy one. Without thinking, without ego, as natural as breathing, he gives his love and he gives himself. In so doing, he expands himself. In living this love, Tim expresses his soul. In loving me for his Self, he has taught me to love him for my Self. As a result, both our lives have expanded; both of us, separately and together, have become more open, trusting, sharing, and interested in the world. Having this degree of love in my life puts me in awe of how unimaginable and uncontainable is God's love for each of us.

How can I recognize my own progress?

The pilgrimage to the soul is not a parade. There are no bands, no spectators, no confetti, and no drama; in short, there is no hoopla. It is not a journey that you would describe as "out of this world" although paradoxically that is where you will go. It is a quiet, often boring journey, and you will not know when you have reached the end. According to the Italian mystic Catherine of Siena, "All the way to Heaven is heaven; we arrive as soon as we depart." You will not find your soul in a moment of great and blinding revelation; it will not jump out at you and make its presence known. Probably, as occurred with my clients, it will reveal its presence to others long before it reveals itself to you. Think of your ego as an exuberant dog and your soul as a contained and demure cat, and you will get the idea.

The soul enters silently into your life, and everything meaningful changes. Your being becomes more important than your doing, and paradoxically you do better. You may think that others have changed because there is more kindness, more gentleness, more visible love, but they are really responding to your change. As time goes by, they too may change, but this is not your concern. You did this journey for yourself, and in the process you have dropped your expectations of them. You began the journey encumbered by all your baggage; along the way you have become lighter and lighter. There are no external souvenirs on this trip, but the internal ones are glorious, and they weigh nothing. The farther along the journey you travel, the more you will let go of, the more unattached and unencumbered you will become. The farther you travel, the more at home you will be. Know that for the ego, there is no right place; for the soul, everywhere and anywhere are the right place to be. Actually for the soul there is no right or wrong; there just is. An Eastern saying describes the process: "First find yourself along the path; then lose yourself and the path is won [One]."

Be careful of melodrama in your journey, for this is the ego asserting itself. This journey is not romantic; it takes place in your mundane, ordinary, everyday life. The soul reveals itself in the most humble daily experiences: a smile, a touch, a moment to listen, a feeling of gratitude, a light in your eyes, a kind word. All this has to begin with yourself and for your Self. It develops in your loving interactions with others, and it culminates in your awareness that God is in all things. You cannot force this experience, or you will subvert it back into the ego's domain. It is even difficult to talk about what you are experiencing without its becoming something special or extraordinary. The best thing to do is let it happen to you in quiet awareness and then share your becoming without explaining how you became. Instead of thinking of yourself as a human being, begin to think of your Self as a being human—always in process.

How do I practice spirituality?

The following exercises are just as simple as your spiritual journey. They are designed to allow you a taste of how this virtue manifests itself. They cannot turn you into a spiritual being—only your relationship with your soul can do that—but they can help you get on the path and stay on it.

Begin by frequently saying the little prayer "Thy will be done" instead of asking for "My will be done." In other words, get out of the driver's seat and allow God to drive you. Trust that He alone holds the master plan and knows what is best for you.

At least once every day try to get into what Taoists call the flow of life. Let yourself go, stop controlling every moment, stop worrying about the outcome, and simply go along for the ride. Stop talking and start listening. Stop telling and start allowing. Suspend all judgments, all evaluations, all criticisms. Just for a little while let things exist as they are without your interference. You might discover that you really like this place. If you hate it, and this exercise is difficult for you, recognize that you have a powerful ego and increase the exercise to three times a day.

Every morning when you are brushing your teeth, choose a number from one to ten. Then perform during the day that amount of acts of kindness. These acts have to be unexpected and something you would not usually do, and they have to involve another living creature. They can be simple and quick—a smile to someone you have never smiled at before, letting someone in line in front of you, slowing down for another car to enter the freeway— or they can be time-consuming—running an errand or doing a favor for someone, giving your dog an extra walk, giving someone your undivided attention for as long as he needs it. Remember, the purpose of these acts is completely selfish; you are doing them for your Self and not for the other. Do not think that you are being of service to them; rather, think that you are taking a service from them, for they are allowing you to perform your acts of kindness.

This next exercise may be the easiest of all; I can attest to the fact that it is the most unusual and, for me, the most powerful. Sing a love song to God. That's right, sing to God to thank Him for His Being; sing to Her to demonstrate your love for Her. Even if you have a terrible voice, as I do, sing away. I discovered this practice from listening to a Ram Dass lecture; he tells of a saintly Indian woman who constantly sings a love song to God. She croons this song when she is alone or in front of hundreds of people. She always sings the same three words: *Ji Om Baghwan*. I love these words even though I'm not sure of their exact meaning; I believe they mean "victory to the One, the Lord." Choose the words that you can feel; perhaps "I love you, God" or "Thank you, my God" or "Thou art my Lord" or whatever conveys your love. Repeat these words over and over, and change the tune as you desire. The important thing is to feel your love for God, and singing aloud seems to make this easier. Also, the repetition lulls the ego and allows the soul to surface. After a while your love song to God will become a love song for everyone; your heart will burst with love. If you don't believe me, try it, but do sing continually for at least one hour. Sing wherever it is possible; the car is a great place. But remember, this is not a performance and should not be too loud or dramatic or you will wake your ego.

Finally, and most critically, look for the humor in everything for it is there. According to author and therapist Thomas Moore, "Wit is a sign of soul." Laugh at yourself. Your ego will hate this as it immediately creates a distance from it. Humor demonstrates detached (from ego) appreciation. Laugh with others—this is spirituality in action—but never at them. It is impossible to feel alienated from others if you can laugh together. Remember, very few things in life are as intense or as serious as your ego will try to make them; your soul knows that there is humor inherent in almost everything.

What is the lesson? A teaching story
This last story is a simple one, which is one of the reasons I chose it to represent the virtue of spirituality. For underneath all the definitions, explanations, and illustrations, behind the complex concepts of virtue, paradox, immanence, and transcendence lies one great and simple truth: Beneath and behind your ego lies your soul; your very being is spiritual.

A LONG TIME AGO in a Far Eastern country there lived a mighty Samurai. His entire life was spent in warring and killing his enemies. Now he has become too old for his previous lifestyle; in his old age he has become interested in questions about death and the meaning of heaven and hell. He decides he had better find out the answers before he dies, so he asks around for someone to tell him the answers he seeks.

He hears of a very wise old monk who lives alone in a desolate monastery. The warrior travels for several days until he comes upon the monastery; upon entering, he finds the old monk deep in meditative prayer.

The Samurai strides boldly and noisily up to the monk, who is obviously irritated to be so rudely disturbed. The monk tersely asks the Samurai, "Why are you disturbing me in my prayers?"

The warrior, not used to being confronted with such a

display of disrespect, becomes furious with the monk. True to fashion, he pulls his sword out of its sheath and raises it over his head in order to strike the monk dead.

Quietly the monk looks at him and says, "That is hell."

The shocked Samurai hesitates and thinks about what the monk has just said. Then he puts his sword down.

Once again the monk speaks: "And that is heaven."

REFERENCES

All definitions of the virtues are based on those in *Webster's New World Dictionary of the American Language.*

Introduction
Michener, James. *Michener's Iberia: Spanish Travels and Reflections, vol. 2.* Great Britain: A Corgi Book, 1983. Pp. 715–21.

Chapter I. Objectivity
Moore, Thomas. *Care of the Soul.* New York: HarperCollins, 1992. Pp. 16–18, 51.
Siddons, Anne Rivers. *Homeplace.* New York: HarperCollins, 1987. P. 289.
Smith, Huston. *The Religions of Man.* New York: Harper & Row, 1958. Pp. 22, 70.
———. *The Wisdom of Faith: Hinduism & Buddhism* video.

Chapter II. Integrity
Bynner, Witter. *The Way of Life According to LaoTzu.* New York: Perigee Books, 1986. Pp. 11–13.
Castaneda, Carlos. *Journey to Ixtlan.* New York: Pocket Books, 1974. P. 168.
Eckhart, Meister, quoted by Paul Zweig. *The Heresy of*

Self-Love. Princeton: Princeton University Press, 1980. Pp. 31–32.

Julian of Norwich. In Brendan Doyle. *Meditations with Julian of Norwich.* Santa Fe: Bear & Co., 1983. P. 61.

O'Connell, Walter "Buzz." "Letting Go and Hanging On: Confessions of a Zen Adlerian." *Individual Psychology,* vol. 40 (1984). Pp. 71–82.

Richie, Donald. *Zen Inklings.* New York: Weatherhill, 1994. Pp. 11–13.

Sanchez, Victor. *The Teachings of Don Carlos.* Santa Fe: Bear & Co., 1995. Pp. 21, 22–24, 25.

Smith, Huston. *The Religions of Man.* New York: Harper & Row, 1958. Pp. 97–109, 181.

———. *The Wisdom of Faith: Hinduism & Buddhism* video.

Chapter III: Morality

Buddha and the mystics, quoted by Paul Zweig. *The Heresy of Self-Love.* Princeton: Princeton University Press, 1980. Pp. 23–34.

Hammerschlag, Carl A., M.D. *The Dancing Healers.* San Francisco: Harper & Row, 1989. P. 146.

Moustakas, Clark. *Loneliness and Love.* Englewood Cliffs, N.J.; Prentice-Hall, 1972. P. 111.

Smith, Huston. *The Religions of Man.* New York: Harper & Row, 1958. Pp. 142–74, 241.

———. *The Wisdom of Faith: Confucianism* video.

Vivekananda, Swami. *Karma-Yoga and Bhakti-Yoga.* New York: Ramakrishna-Vivekananda Center, 1973. P. 15.

Chapter IV: Creativity

Campbell, Joseph, quoted by D. K. Osborn. *Reflections on the Art of Living: A Joseph Campbell Companion.* New York: HarperCollins, 1991. P. 75.

Csikszentmihalyi, Mihaly. *Creativity.* New York: HarperCollins, 1996. Pp. 20–23, 57, 75–84.

Moustakas, Clark. *Loneliness and Love.* Englewood Cliffs, N.J.: Prentice-Hall, 1972. Pp. 4–5.

O'Connell, W., and E. Gomez. "Dialectics, Trances, and the Wisdom of Encouragement," *Individual Psychology,* vol. 46 (1990). Pp. 431–42.

Smith, Huston. *The Religions of Man.* New York: Harper & Row, 1958. Pp. 181–88, 223, 225–65.

Stern, Richard, quoted by Mihaly Csikszentmihalyi. *Creativity,* loc. cit. Pp. 119–20.

Vivekananda, Swami. *Karma-Yoga and Bhakti-Yoga.* New York: Ramakrishna-Vivekananda Center, 1973. P. 20.

Walsch, Neale Donald. *Conversations with God: An Uncommon Dialogue.* Charlottesville, Va: Hampton Roads Publishing, 1995. Pp. 52–54, 74–75.

Chapter V: Spontaneity

Bolen, Jean Shinoda. *The Tao of Psychology: Synchronicity and the Self.* San Francisco: Harper & Row Publications, 1982. P. 99.

Bynner, Witter. *The Way of Life According to LaoTzu.* New York: Perigee Books, 1986. P. 42.

cummings, e. e., quoted by L. G. Boldt. *Zen and the Art of*

Making a Living. New York: Arkana/Penguin, 1993. P. 231.

Frank, Frederick, quoted by Jean Bolen. *The Tao of Psychology,* loc. cit. Pp. 2–3.

Levine, Stephen, and Ram Dass. *From Tragedy to Grace/ The Experience of Dying.* Videotape produced by Original Face Video in the Hanuman Foundation Video Library, 1981.

May, Rollo. *The Courage to Create.* New York: Norton, 1975. Pp. 13–14.

O'Connell, W., and E. Hooker. "Anxiety Disorders II." In L. Sperry and J. Carlson, eds. *Psychopathology and Psychotherapy.* Washington, D.C.: Accelerated Development, 1996. Pp. 179–220.

Smith, Huston. *The Religions of Man.* New York: Harper & Row, 1958. Pp. 175–92.

Strand, Mark. *Creativity.* Mihaly Csikszentmihalyi. New York, HarperCollins, 1996. P. 121.

Walsch, Neale Donald. *Conversations with God: An Uncommon Dialogue.* Charlottesville, Va. Hampton Roads Publishing, 1995. Pp. 65, 18–19, 66, 98.

Chapter VI: Generosity
Boldt, Laurence G. *Zen and the Art of Making a Living.* New York: Arkana/Penguin Books, 1993. P. 236. (Note: All the quotations cited in the section "How can I balance my head with my heart?" are from this book.)

Campbell, Joseph. *The Power of Myth.* New York: Doubleday, 1988. P. 41. Also quoted by L. G. Boldt. *Zen and the Art of Making a Living,* loc. cit. Pp. 53, 80.

Gandhi, Mahatma, quoted by Ram Dass. *Cultivating Mindfulness/Wisdom Has No Fear of Death.* Videotape produced by Original Face Video in the Hanuman Foundation Video Library, 1981.

Hua-Ching No. *Hua Hu Ching: The Later Teachings of Lao Tzu.* Boston: Shambhala, 1995. P. 8.

Levine, Stephen. *From Tragedy to Grace/The Experience of Dying.* Videotape produced by Original Face Video in the Hanuman Foundation Video Library, 1981.

O'Connell, Walter "Buzz." "Natural High Theory and Practice: A Psychospiritual Integration." *Journal of Integrative and Eclectic Psychotherapy* (1988), Pp. 441–54.

Ram Dass. *Cultivating Mindfulness/Wisdom Has No Fear of Death.* Videotape produced by Original Face Video in the Hanuman Foundation Video Library, 1981.

Smith, Huston. *The Religions of Man.* New York: Harper & Row, 1958. Pp. 193–224.

———. In *The Wisdom of Faith: Islam* video.

Suzuki, Shunryu. *Zen Mind, Beginner's Mind.* New York: Weatherhill, 1993.

Vivekananda, Swami. *Karma-Yoga and Bhakti-Yoga.* New York: Ramakrishna-Vivekananda Center, 1955. P. 39.

Walsch, Neale Donald. *Conversations with God: An Uncommon Dialogue.* Charlottesville, Va.: Hampton Roads Publishing, 1995. P. 19.

Zen Buddhist poem describing satori, cited by Smith. *The Religions of Man,* loc. cit. P. 134.

Chapter VII: Spirituality

Adler, Alfred. In W. E. O'Connell. *Essential Readings in Natural High Actualization.* Chicago: North American Graphics, 1981. Pp. 1–15.

Blyth, R. H. In J. S. Bolen, *The Tao of Psychology: Synchronicity and the Self.* San Francisco: Harper & Row, 1979. P. 9.

Campbell, Joseph. In D. K. Osborn, ed. *Reflections on the Art of Living: A Joseph Campbell Companion.* New York: HarperCollins, 1991. P. 173.

Catherine of Siena, quoted by James P. Carse. *Breakfast at the Victory: The Mysticism of Ordinary Experience.* San Francisco: Harper, 1994. P. 39.

Eckhart, Meister (first citation), quoted by Joseph Campbell. *Reflections on the Art of Living,* loc. cit. P. 168.

————. (second citation), quoted by Larry Dossey. *Recovering the Soul: A Scientific and Spiritual Search.* New York: Bantam Books, 1989. P. 48.

Fox, Matthew, and Rupert Sheldrake. From an interview, Richard Scheinin, "Science and Spirituality," Knight-Ridder Newspapers, January 1996.

Julian of Norwich. In Brendon Doyle, *Meditations with Julian of Norwich.* Santa Fe: Bear & Co., 1993. Pp. 59, 119.

Lao-tzu, quoted by Alan Watts. *Tao: The Watercourse Way*. New York: Pantheon Books, 1975. P. 108.

Moore, Thomas. From an interview entitled "Mind of a Soul Man." *Mixed Media* (November–December 1996). Pp. 90–91.

O'Connell, Walter "Buzz." "Radical Metaphors of Adlerian Psychospirituality." *Individual Psychology*, vol. 53 (1997). Pp. 33–41.

———. "Natural High Theory and Practice: The Humorist's Game of Games." In W. Fry and W. Salameh, eds. *Handbook of Humor and Psychotherapy: Advances in the Clinical Use of Humor*. Sarasota, Fla.: Professional Resources Exchange, 1987. Pp. 55–79.

Peck, M. Scott. *Further Along the Road Less Traveled*. New York: Simon & Schuster, 1993. P. 94.

Ram Dass. *Cultivating Mindfulness/Wisdom Has No Fear of Death*. Videotape produced by Original Face Video in the Hanuman Foundation Video Library, 1981.

Smith, Huston. *The Religions of Man*. New York: Harper & Row, 1958. Pp. 266–308.

———. *The Wisdom of Faith: A Personal Philosophy* video.

Williamson, Marianne. *A Return to Love: Reflections on the Principles of a Course in Miracles*. New York: Harper Perennial, 1993. Pp. 137, 157.

The Pilgrim's Hymn

Who would true valour see,
Let him come hither;
One here will constant be,
Come wind, come weather;
There's no discouragement
Shall make him once relent
His first avowed intent
To be a pilgrim.

Who so beset him round
With dismal stories,
Do but themselves confound;
His strength the more is.
No lion can him fright;
He'll with a giant fight,
But he will have the right
To be a pilgrim.

No goblin nor foul fiend
Can daunt his spirit;
He knows he at the end
Shall life inherit.
Then, fancies, fly away;
He'll not fear what men say;
He'll labour night and day
To be a pilgrim.

—John Bunyan